Arias, Cabalettas, and Foreign Affairs

To Susie
with warm regards

Hans L. Tuch
11-08

Memoirs and Occasional Papers
Association for Diplomatic Studies and Training

In 2003, the Association for Diplomatic Studies and Training (ADST) created the Memoirs and Occasional Papers Series to preserve firsthand accounts and other informed observations on foreign affairs for scholars, journalists, and the general public. Sponsoring publication of the series is one of numerous ways in which ADST, a nonprofit organization founded in 1986, seeks to promote understanding of American diplomacy and those who conduct it. Together with the Foreign Affairs Oral History program and ADST's support for the training of foreign affairs personnel at the State Department's Foreign Service Institute, these efforts constitute the Association's fundamental purposes.

J. Chapman Chester
FROM FOGGY BOTTOM TO CAPITOL HILL
Exploits of a G.I., Diplomat, and Congressional Aide

Robert E. Gribbin
IN THE AFTERMATH OF GENOCIDE
The U.S. Role in Rwanda

Allen C Hansen
NINE LIVES: A Foreign Service Odyssey

James R. Huntley
AN ARCHITECT OF DEMOCRACY
Building a Mosaic of Peace

John G. Kormann
ECHOES OF A DISTANT CLARION
Recollections of a Diplomat and Soldier

Armin Meyer
QUIET DIPLOMACY
From Cairo to Tokyo in the Twilight of Imperialism

William Morgan and Charles Stuart Kennedy, eds.
AMERICAN DIPLOMATS: The Foreign Service at Work

James M. Potts
FRENCH COVERT ACTION
IN THE AMERICAN REVOLUTION

Daniel Whitman
A HAITI CHRONICLE
The Undoing of a Latent Democracy

Arias, Cabalettas, and Foreign Affairs

A Public Diplomat's
Quasi-Musical Memoir

Hans N. Tuch

Association for Diplomatic Studies and Training
Memoirs and Occasional Papers Series

Washington, DC

The views and opinions in this book are solely those of the author and not necessarily those of the Association for Diplomatic Studies and Training or the United States government.

VELLUM/New Academia Publishing, 2008

Printed in the United States of America

Library of Congress Control Number: 2008931607
ISBN 978-0-9818654-0-9 paperback (alk. paper)

To my wife, Mimi,
who has enthusiastically and discerningly shared my love for
opera and, patiently and loyally, my life in diplomacy.

Other Books by Hans N. Tuch

Atoms at Your Service (with Henry A. Dunlap)
New York: Harper & Brothers, 1957.

Arthur Burns and the Successor Generation
Lanham, MD: University Press of America, 1988.

Communicating wih the World: U.S. Public Diplomacy Overseas
New York: St. Martin's Press, 1990.

I haven't understood a bar of music in my life, but I have felt it.
— Stravinsky

Contents

Acknowledgments

I have tremendous appreciation for ADST Publishing Director Margery Thompson's ability as an editor, and I thank her for again making the proverbial sow's ear into a silk purse. She was ably and imaginatively assisted by ADST interns Dilanthi Ranaweera, Kaitlin Leary, and Anjan Mukherjee.

I am grateful to Susan Weinsheimer, the librarian and archivist of the Wolf Trap Opera Company, who initially computerized my collection of opera, concert, and theater programs, for checking the facts in this book, a major task.

I deeply appreciate the artistry demonstrated by Debra Murov in her cover design for this volume. I thank our friend Sylvia Weiss for guiding me safely through the shoals of operating a new computer. And, finally, I appreciate my friend and colleague Len Baldyga's efforts in spreading the word about this publication.

Prelude

I start this book with a disclaimer: I am neither a musician nor a musicologist. I am merely a lover of opera, and of music in general. I approach my experiences over seventy years with opera and classical music, and my acquaintance with musical artists in many countries of the world, primarily as a memoir in the context of my life in diplomacy.

I define myself as an opera buff, as a person who loves opera as an art form but is neither a professional nor an expert in the field. An opera buff like me attends performances whenever and wherever he can and repeats attendance at the same operas on many occasions. He talks, reads, breathes opera and appears to those who don't share this enthusiasm as a person of strange tastes and mannerisms (especially if he is the type who cannot help "conducting" with his fingers, hand, or even forearm as he sits watching and listening in the opera house).

In my case, it was partly a matter of upbringing. My mother, a woman of cultivated and liberal tradition, did not force me to take music lessons (and thus I have played no instrument well), but she inculcated in me a love of music. My father, a practical man, did not interfere; he even claimed that I showed musical talent at an early age since I cried whenever my mother sang. But that turned out to be a family joke, for my mother had a lovely, trained voice.

I did seem to have a high boy-soprano voice, which was trained over a period of six months by our local cantor to sing the entire bar mitzvah service in the temple on my thirteenth birthday. My one "semiprofessional" appearance was judged successful—at least by my family and their invited friends—but it also marked the beginning and end of my singing career; the following year my voice changed, and I was no longer able to voice a true note.

At any rate, my mother began my musical education wisely with tunes like the Triumphal March from *Aida*, the Anvil Chorus from

Il Trovatore, and the Toreador's Song from *Carmen*. I thus slid into the artform the easy way—through 78 rpm records of highlights from the most singable and popular operas.

Berlin—1938

In the early fall of 1938 I was permitted to attend my first opera performance at the famed Berlin Staatsoper, the premier opera house in Germany and, at the time, one of the world's grandest. The opera, carefully chosen by my mother, was Gounod's *Faust*, selected partly because I was familiar with Göthe's tale, partly because I already knew some of its most singable tunes.

The way ordinary folks obtained tickets for seats in the upper reaches of the Staatsoper in those days was to stand in line early on Sunday morning when tickets went on sale for the following week. I considered myself lucky to be successful on my first try. The following Thursday my mother, who had been widowed two years before, and I, her thirteen-year old son, climbed to the third *Rang*—the third gallery above the orchestra and the tier of boxes— where we had seats in the first row on the side, looking straight down onto the orchestra pit and stage.

It was a memorable performance, made so by artists regarded as among the world's finest singers, who enjoyed a popularity akin to that of today's pop stars. The great lyric soprano Maria Müller sang the title role (Gounod's opera was known as *Margarete* in Germany, not *Faust*). Helge Roswaenge sang the role of Faust, Heinrich Schlussnuss was Valentin, and Ludwig Hoffmann was Mephistopheles—as stellar a cast as could be assembled in an opera house in those days. (They were the Kiri Te Kanawa, Placido Domingo, Sherrill Milnes, and Nikolai Ghiaurov of their day.)

My introduction to the world of live opera was quickly followed by several other performances. The reason for this haste was that I was shortly to be sent to America to live with relatives in the Midwest, which to any German schoolboy was notably the land of Indians and cowboys (indelibly imprinted into his psyche by that most notorious of German adventure book authors Karl May), and not the land of Verdi and Mozart. To save my budding musical soul, therefore, my second live opera performance, again in the Staatsoper, was Verdi's *Il Trovatore*, with almost the same cast as in the *Faust* performance, including again Maria Müller, Helge Roswaenge, and Heinrich Schlussnuss, plus the fine contralto Margarete Klose as Azucena.

On the third occasion I "graduated" to Wagner. The Staatsoper's *Tannhäuser* was for this 13-year old a thrilling performance,

My fourth opera performance: Program of the Staatsoper, Fidelio. Herbert von Karajan's first appearance in the Staatsoper. (Wolf Trap Collection).

featuring the fabled Tiana Lemnitz as Elisabet, Germany's leading heroic tenor, Franz Völker, as Tannhäuser and, again, Heinrich Schlussnuss, as Wolfram von Eschenbach. Schlussnuss was a superb lyric baritone, unrivaled in those days as both a Lieder and an opera singer.

The final performance I attended in Berlin, shortly before leaving for the United States in October 1938, was the Staatsoper's *Fidelio*. And that performance, as it turned out, was historic. (To explain, I must digress for a moment. I have collected opera, concert, and recital programs ever since I started going to performances. Most of the information and specific data in this book are derived from these programs or at least confirmed by them. Unfortunately, the programs of the first three Staatsoper performances recalled above were lost, but the one of Beethoven's *Fidelio* is still part of the collection.[1])

I remember looking at the program and being somewhat disappointed that the conductor was an unknown, making a guest appearance. Only years later, when I glanced at the program again, did I discover that the unheralded guest conductor of that performance had been Herbert von Karajan, who, I learned, made his Berlin debut on that September 30, 1938, coming from the provincial opera house in Aachen, where he was conducting at that time.

Kansas City

Kansas City in the late 1930s and 1940s had no opera house, but the Saturday afternoon Metropolitan Opera broadcasts were a worthy substitute for this young opera buff. While most of my friends were out playing sandlot football, I was glued to the radio, often together with two friends with similar tastes: Ed Kander, who served many years later as development director of the Kansas City Lyric Opera, and his younger brother, John, who turned out to be a musician and composer of great talent. John and his partner Fred Ebb—the team of Kander and Ebb—created such musicals as *Cabaret, Chicago, Kiss of the Spider Woman, Zorba, Woman of the Year, The Rink,* and many others.

I have an old *Victor Book of the Opera* and recorded in it some of the opera casts that we heard in these performances between 1938 and 1943. It seems amazing now that such great artists of that era as Ezio Pinza, Jussi Bjoerling, Lawrence Tibbett, Helen Jepson, Elizabeth Rethberg, Bidu Sayao, John Brownlee, Jarmila Novotna, Eleanor Steber, Zinka Milanov, Jan Pearce, Lily Pons, Grace Moore, and many more appeared regularly on these broadcasts.

With my aunt and uncle I attended all the subscription concerts of the Kansas City Philharmonic, under a somewhat mediocre conductor, Karl Krüger (even then I recognized this!).Two stand out in my memory (and the programs are in my collection). One was a concert featuring the great pianist Artur Schnabel playing the Beethoven First and the Mozart B-flat (K595) piano concertos; the other was a concert featuring the wonderful soprano Helen Jepson singing works by Rachmaninoff and Delius. I, of course, immediately fell in love with Helen Jepson, and her only competition for my affections was the lovely Gladys Swarthout, whom I heard on Met broadcasts but never saw.

As a newly minted American teenager, I immediately learned to love popular music by way of the big bands—Glenn Miller, Tommy and Jimmy Dorsey, Artie Shaw, and Benny Goodman. In Kasas City jazz became a primary passion. My cousin Geoff and I used to sneak out at night and drive down to 12th Street, the K.C. jazz mecca, to listen to Harlan Leonard and his band at the College Inn. (Living on the Kansas side of the border, in what is now Shawnee Mission, we were able to acquire driver's licenses at age 14.) The band's drummer, Jesse Price, became Geoff's percussion teacher. I learned to play trombone and was pretty bad at it, never progressing beyond the high school marching band and orchestra and a small jazz combo. I finally gave up on the instrument and later sold it to buy my fiancee an engagement ring.

In May 1943, I was drafted into the Army. I had one memorable musical experience while being trained for overseas duty at the University of Illinois. I attended a recital at the university by the great Wagnerian soprano Helen Traubel, an occasion that has stayed with me to this day.

Because of my service as a paratrooper in the 101st Airborne Division—I was an intelligence specialist, an interrogator of POWs—I gained enough combat "points" to get out of the Army by December 1945 and return home to resume my studies at the University of Kansas City (now the University of Missouri–Kansas City).

Music or Diplomacy?

I was lucky in that I came to the realization early on that, although I loved music, I had no real talent or ear for a career in music. So I majored in history and political science (taking music courses as electives for pleasure), received my bachelor of arts degree in 1947, and went directly for a master of arts in international relations at the School of Advanced International Studies (SAIS—subsequently

The author as paratrooper in World War II: Berchtesgaden, May 1945, just after V-E Day.

to become part of Johns Hopkins University) in Washington, D.C. A second stroke of luck was that I met my future wife, Ruth Marie (Mimi) Lord, at SAIS in 1947.

A third stroke of luck, as will be evident throughout this narrative, was that my eventual career as a U.S. Foreign Service officer enabled me to connect diplomacy with my love of opera, and of music in general, during many of the next thirty-five years. (Some of my friends claim that I never accepted a post without an opera house, citing Frankfurt, Munich, Moscow, Sofia, Berlin, Rio de Janeiro, and Bonn as evidence, but they forget that we also spent four years in Brasilia.)

One musical experience that occurred while I was still a student merits special mention. In 1947 the School of Advanced International Studies had a summer program in Peterboro, New Hampshire, in the facilities of a girls' boarding school. While there, we students took advantage of the proximity of the McDowell Colony, where composers and musicians in residence frequently offered informal recitals.

Our Russian teacher, Madame Toumanova, a traditional but personable elderly Russian émigrée from the Soviet revolution, owned a turkey farm in the vicinity and, incongruously, drove a pickup truck. She invited several of her students to drive over to Tanglewood one weekend, where we heard two concerts by the Boston Symphony under Serge Koussevitsky.

One concert featured Beethoven's First, Second and Third Symphonies, and the other consisted of the Brahms Second Symphony and compositions by Honnegger and Debussy. This was my first hearing of the Boston Symphony under its famed music director. The atmosphere of Tanglewood—the wide green lawn, the sunny weather, the informal but attentive crowd, and the wonderful music—all added to the enjoyment and lasting memory of this occasion.

My first job after graduation was as an international trainee at the Chase National Bank in New York, a prestigious but paternalistic institution. I was paid very little—the bank considered it a privilege to be a part of it— and living in New York was expensive even then, though the bank provided lunches, my main meal. I found plenty to enjoy, nonetheless, in the many free concerts available. Two stand out in my memory. One was a Sunday afternoon recital by the cellist Gregor Piatigorsky in the Frick Gallery. I remember that concert vividly—beside the wonderful cello playing—inasmuch as I had been unaware of Piatigorsky's habit of spitting while he played. Having innocently secured a seat in the first row, I was

☆   ☆

BERKSHIRE FESTIVAL...TENTH SEASON, 1947

Boston Symphony Orchestra

SERGE KOUSSEVITZKY, *Music Director*

Sixth Program

Thursday Evening, July 31, *at* 8:15

BEETHOVEN . . . . Symphony No. 1 in C major, *Op.* 21

   I. Adagio molto; Allegro con brio   III. Menuetto: Allegro molto e vivace

   II. Andante cantabile con moto   IV. Finale: Adagio; Allegro molto e vivace

BEETHOVEN . . . . Symphony No. 2 in D major, *Op.* 36

   I. Adagio molto; allegro con brio   III. Scherzo

   II. Larghetto   IV. Allegro molto

INTERMISSION

BEETHOVEN . . . . . . Symphony No. 3 in E-flat major, "Eroica," *Op.* 55

   I. Allegro con brio   III. Scherzo: Allegro vivace; Trio

   II. Marcia funebre: Adagio assai   IV. Finale: Allegro

BALDWIN PIANO   VICTOR RECORDS

*Program of the Tanglewood Festival Concert by the Boston Symphony
under Serge Koussevitzky, July 1947 (Wolf Trap Collection)*

repeatedly sprayed by the artist's saliva, especially during his most intensive playing.

The other musical event of vivid memory was a Saturday concert by the NBC Symphony under Arturo Toscanini, my one and only occasion to hear and see the great maestro. One had to stand in line to obtain a free ticket, and I managed to get a good seat where I could watch the conductor close up. Unfortunately, I have no program of either concert, so memory must serve to recall my enjoyment of the music that was made. I attended two performances at the Old Met during the winter of 1949: Charpentier's *Louise* and Richard Strauss's *Salome*. I have no proof of programs of these performances. Not being able to afford the price of admission to the Met, the ticket must have been provided by my cousin, "Uncle" Julius, who came to New York several times a year from Kansas City on business and usually took me to dinner and the theater or opera. My only evidence of witnessing these productions is my vivid memory of hearing the wonderful Dorothy Kirsten as Louise and the overpowering—both vocally and physically—Ljuba Welitsch as Salome in my first witnessing of these operas.

During this time, Mimi was an intelligence analyst in the super-secret Army Security Agency in Arlington, Virginia, and we exchanged biweekly visits on weekends. On one Saturday in January 1949 in New York, we managed to get standing-room tickets for *Kiss Me Kate,* which had just opened to rave reviews. We loved this Cole Porter work, and its many wonderful melodies and delightful lyrics became, in a way, "our" musical. We have seen it several times since, but even some of the star-studded productions we have attended can't erase the memories of that first performance with Alfred Drake, Lisa Kirk, Patricia Morison, and Harold Lang, with Hanya Holm's choreography. *Kiss Me Kate* ranks with *Westside Story* and *My Fair Lady* as my candidates for American musical theater's finest.

My employment with the bank was short-lived. Dispatched to Stuttgart to work in one of the bank's branches in Germany, I was able to find hard-to-obtain living accommodations and announced my intention to bring my fiancée over so that we could get married. At this point the bank informed me that I could not get married for three years so that the bank could move me around the country to one or another of the its branches. Talk of paternalism!

I walked out of the bank without having enough money to return to the United States. Luckily, the Department of State was at that moment taking over from the Military Government the administration of U.S. affairs in Germany. I applied for a job at HICOG (High Commissioner for Occupied Germany) in Frankfurt in any field other than finance. I was referred to the director of the America House program, a Mrs. Patricia van Delden, in nearby Bad Nauheim. I had never heard of the program and did not know what an America House was, but I took my chance and appeared in Mrs. Van Delden's office for an interview, where I was ushered into the office of her deputy, Max Kimental. As soon as we started talking, he excused himself to take a phone call and suggested I make myself comfortable and read whatever I found on his coffee table.

I noticed a three-page paper by Patricia van Delden entitled, "The Future of the America House Program," which I quickly perused. Kimental returned and, starting the interview, asked what I would want to accomlish the next year if I were an America House director. As I regurgitated what I had just read, he stopped me after two minutes and excused himself again. He returned with Patricia van Delden, an attractive but formidable lady in her midforties. She asked me to repeat what I had started to say, so I continued with what I remembered of her account (without, of course, attributing the source).

The result: I was sworn into the Foreign Service that day and assigned to be the director of the Wiesbaden America House. So began my "distinguished" diplomatic career. (It took me two years to admit to Mrs. Van Delden how I had been so articulate in my interview.)

During my few months in Stuttgart the opera was going full blast—literally—as it had to share its building with a USO service club. Thus, while listening to the music of, say, *Tosca*, one also heard the rhythmic ping-ponging of a table tennis match in action and the jukebox playing popular tunes.

I nevertheless attended several performances during which I first heard the famous Wagnerian tenor Wolfgang Windgassen in a number of roles, but I shall recall here only one production of Mozart's *Magic Flute*. A mezzo-soprano named Mildred Müller, who sang the role of the Third Lady-in-Waiting. was in fact Mildred Miller at the beginning of her career. She was later to become a mainstay of the Metropolitan Opera, praised especially for her role as Cherubino in *The Marriage of Figaro*. (I shall come back to her in a later chapter.)

ACT I
The Foreign Service, Years 1949–1985

1

Germany 1949–1955

Now to the serious business of being a young Foreign Service officer (FSO) and to my first assignment as cultural affairs officer and director of a U.S.cultural and information center, first, briefly in Wiesbaden (1949–50) and then, for five years, in Frankfurt (1950–55).

Wiesbaden at that time housed the Central Collecting Point, where many of the artworks dislocated as the result of Nazi confiscations, wartime looting, safeguarding, and hiding were being collected, secured, and catalogued pending further disposition. One day I was visiting my senior colleague Edgar Breitenbach, who served as director of the Collecting Point, as he unpacked a large crate. He suddenly said, "You'll want to hold this, but don't drop it," and handed me the world-renowned limestone bust of the Egyptian queen Nefertiti, described by Baedeker as "one of the most lifelike portraits in the whole period [1375–1350 BC] of Egyptian art." It is probably now the main attraction in Berlin's Egyptian Museum. I remember my shock at actually holding this world treasure in my hands and promising myself to tell the tale someday.

Frankfurt

Like most of the major German cities at the time, Frankfurt in 1950 remained almost completely destroyed as the result of World War II. The educational and cultural infrastructure was nonexistent—libraries, theaters, concert halls, and the university were in rubble. The U.S. government early on realized that in order to help Germany reestablish itself as a viable democratic society, it had to reconnect the German people with the West through culture and education as well as politically, economically, and socially. U.S. cultural and information centers (known locally as Amerika Häuser) served initially as local community centers in the absence of the destroyed German cultural institutions.

In Frankfurt, the America House consisted of a library of about 45,000 American books in English and in German translation and a large collection of periodicals. At the time, it was the only public library in the city and was open seven days a week from 10 a.m. to 10 p.m., served by a staff of twenty-five trained German librarians. Most important, it was also the first ever open-shelf library in the city. The main impact of the America Houses, according to one German researcher, was "in influencing and changing the view of America among the German people. Through the medium of the library it was possible to persuade Germans to regard America positively and often admiringly."[2]

In connection with the library, the America House featured exhibitions, English language classes, nightly lectures and discussions, and, most important in the context of this memoir, weekly recitals and chamber music concerts by young American artists. I was the only American in the Center, and the job entailed both administering a busy institution with a staff of forty-five Germans and dealing with books, art, and musical performing artists. I could not have imagined a more fulfilling employment and life—sharing it with the woman I loved.

Mimi and I, I should interject here, were married in Wiesbaden in December 1949, first in the German *Standesamt*, the legal ceremony, and the next morning in the U.S. Air Force's Camp Lindsay Chapel by an Air Force Chaplain—that ceremony considered by Mimi the operative one because at this one she understood what was happening.

Among the many outstanding American musicians who performed in the Frankfurt America House were the pianists Leon Fleischer, Ned Rorem, and Grant Johannesen; cellist Madeline Foley; organist E. Power Biggs; and Hans Ulrich Schnabel (son of Artur), who with his wife, Helen Schnabel, played four-handed piano recitals. Some of them came over from Paris, where they belonged to Nadia Boulanger's circle of young musicians and composers. They played for a pittance, only a D-Mark per-diem equivalent to $10 per day, sweetened often by a home-cooked meal prepared by my wife.

I will always remember the morning Leon Fleischer arrived and I handed him his accumulated mail. The first envelope he opened was his U.S. Army draft notice, which he threw back at me with an appropriate expletive. Though I have had no personal contact with Fleischer since then, I heard his excellent musicianship with the Juilliard Quartet at the Library of Congress in the 1960s and recently

The American organist E. Power Biggs performed in Frankfurt in 1953 under the auspices of the America House (U.S. Information Service).

with the National Symphony Orchestra, playing Beethoven's Emperor Concerto. I can only say, "I knew him when!" He was marvelous then, as he is now.

The Juilliard Quartet came to Frankfurt in 1952 to perform under the auspices of the America House. After the concert, I transported Robert Mann, the first violinist, in my car to our apartment, where Mimi had prepared a small supper for the artists and some friends. I never locked my car because, if I had done so, it would have been broken into. What I did not know was that Mann had left his violin in the open car, and when we returned later the priceless Guadanini instrument (belonging to the Juilliard School) had been stolen.

What to do? We sat up all night with the police trying to determine how to proceed: whether to publicize the theft, in which case the instrument would probably disappear forever into East Germany; or keep quiet, thereby speculating that the thief did not know the value of what he had stolen and might dispose of it locally. The latter plan fortunately prevailed, and the instrument was found two days later, having been sold for DM48.00 ($12.00) in a hockshop on Frankfurt's main thoroughfare.

Nerves were frazzle and nails obliterated, but one happy ending begot another: a lifelong friendship was begun that night with the Juillard's violist, Rafael Hillyer.

Another, less critical crisis occurred when the young American cembalist, Daniel Pinkham, disappeared just as his much anticipated recital in the America House was about to start. We searched all over but could not find him. We had already solved one major problem when his cembalo failed to arrive—it had been left in Nuremberg by mistake—and we had to find a replacement in Frankfurt, not an easy task in those days. Now the artist had vanished. Suddenly we heard cries for help emanating from an upstairs bathroom. It turned out that the lock had broken as he tried to leave. Even an urgently summoned locksmith was unable to open the door. In the end, the use of an axe became the only solution so that Pinkham could finally emerge to concertize.

In the early 1950s, Mimi and I were able to see many opera performances and hear numerous concerts and recitals in Wiesbaden, Frankfurt, and elsewhere. In Wiesbaden in 1950 we heard the Berlin Philharmonic under Wilhelm Furtwängler for the first time. This magnificent ensemble played the Bruckner Seventh Symphony on that occasion. At another time we heard the famed violinist Adolf Busch play the Beethoven Violin Concerto with the Hessian Symphony Orchestra under Ludwig Kaufmann, a good conductor who was also the music director of the Hessian State Opera in Wiesbaden at the time. Under his baton we heard eleven opera performances in 1950–51, during which we were introduced to our first *Samson and Dalila, Falstaff, Pelleas and Melisande, Rosenkavalier, Forza del destino,* and *Magic Flute.*

In Frankfurt that year, a chamber music concert in a makeshift hall remains in my memory. It featured the pianist Edwin Fischer, the violinist Wolfgang Schneiderhahn, and the cellist Enrico Mainardi.

During those two years our vacation travels and officially sanctioned trips within Germany, as well as to Austria and Switzerland, gave Mimi and me the opportunity to hear some wonderful music. (It was only after December 1951, when our son David was born in Frankfurt that our travel schedule—at least Mimi's—became more circumscribed.)

One weekend found us in Bern, hearing Inge Borkh singing *Electra,* a new opera for us. In 1950, on my first trip back to Berlin since leaving in 1938, we heard the Berlin Philharmonic under Bruno Walter play the Mozart G-Minor Symphony in addition to Beethoven and Richard Strauss compositions. Vienna was our destination that Easter. There, at the Gesellschaft der Musikfreunde,

DEUTSCHE STAATSOPER

Sonntag, den 24. Juni 1951

Der Rosenkavalier

Komödie für Musik in 3 Akten von Hugo von Hofmannsthal

Musik von Richard Strauß

Musikalische Leitung: Erich Kleiber

Inszenierung: Wolf Völker

Bühnenbilder: Lothar Schenck von Trapp

Die Feldmarschallin Fürstin Werdenberg . . . . Tiana Lemnitz
Der Baron Ochs auf Lerchenau . . . . Theo Herrmann a. G.
Oktavian, genannt Quinquin, ein junger Herr aus großem Haus . . . . Anneliese Müller
Herr von Faninal, ein reicher Neugeadelter . . . . Kurt Rehm
Sophie, seine Tochter . . . . Elfride Trötschel
Jungfer Marianne Leitmetzerin, die Duenna . . . . .Hildegard Lüdtke
Valzacchi, ein Intrigant . . . . Paul Schmidtmann
Annina, seine Begleiterin . . . . Karola Goerlich
Ein Polizeikommissar . . . . Eugen Fuchs
Der Haushofmeister bei der Feldmarschallin . . . . Walter Stoll
Der Haushofmeister bei Faninal . . . . .Heinz Braun
Ein Notar . . . . Kay Willumsen
Ein Wirt . . . . Fritz Soot
Ein Sänger . . . . Rudolf Schock
Eine Modistin . . . . Jolanda Szalai
Ein Tierhändler . . . . .Heinz Braun
Leopold . . . . Rolf Wölfle
Ein Hausdiener . . . . Ludwig Buch
Lakaien der Marschallin . . . . Th. Westerhold, G. Reimer, K. Ronneburg, G. Hintze
Drei adlige Waisen . . . . .A. Goos, W. Reinhart, H. Scharrer

Ein kleiner Neger · ein Gelehrter · ein Flötist · ein Friseur, dessen Gehilfe · eine adlige
Witwe · eine Kammerfrau · ein Verwalter · ein Koch · Bediente Lerchenaus · Läuter
Heiducken · Küchenpersonal · ein Arzt · Kellner · Gäste · zwei Wächter · Kinder
Musikanten · Kutscher · verdächtige Gestalten · Lakaien

In Wien in den ersten Jahren der Regierung Maria Theresias

Kostümgestaltung: Kurt Palm
Technische Leitung: Max Hübner
Inspizient: Géza Gurnik

PAUSE NACH DEM 1. UND 2. AKT

Program of the Berlin Staatsoper: Der Rosenkavalier, *conducted by Erich Kleiber and featuring Tiana Lemnitz as the Marschallin, with Anneliese Müller and Elfride Trötschel, and Rudolf Schock as the "Sänger," June 1951 (Wolf Trap Collection).*

we heard the Vienna Philharmonic under Eugen Jochum perform Bach's St. John's Passion, with the soloists Irmgard Seefried, Julius Patzak, Hans Braun, and Otto Edelmann.

Again in Berlin in 1951, we were able to hear a wonderful performance in the Staatsoper (in its temporary location in the Admiralspalast) of *Der Rosenkavalier*, under the baton of Erich Kleiber, with soprano Tiana Lemnitz, by then legendary, as the Marschallin. (I remembered hearing her at the Berlin Staatsoper when I was thirteen, shortly before I left for the United States.)

I first attended the Salzburg Festival in 1949, and again in 1950 with Mimi. Tickets were then still easily available and affordable. In 1950 we were able to find wonderful accommodations at Schloss Fuschl on Lake Fuschl, a few miles from Salzburg, where a former Nazi minister had built himself a beautiful summer chalet that after the war had been converted into a small luxurious hotel.

In 1949 alone, I heard a magnificent performance of *Fidelio*, conducted by Furtwängler, with Kirsten Flagstad in the title role, plus Irmgard Seefried, Julius Patzak, Paul Schöffler, and Anton Dermota. I also attended a concert by the Vienna Philharmonic under Bruno Walter performing Mahler's *Das Lied von der Erde* with the great Kathleen Ferrier and Julius Patzak.

In 1950, Mimi and I heard *Fidelio*, again under Furtwängler with the same cast as in 1949, except that Elisabet Schwarzkopf sang the role of Marzeline.

The next night we heard a great *Don Giovanni*, again under Furtwängler, with Tito Gobbi, Lyuba Welich, Elisabet Schwarzkopf, Irmgard Seefried, Erich Kunz, Anton Dermota, and Josef Greindl. We also attended a beautiful performance of the Brahms German Requiem, conducted by Joseph Messner, with Irmgard Seefried and Paul Schöffler.

On a vacation trip to Italy in 1951, we visited Florence, and upon arrival saw a poster of the *Maggio Musicale*, the May Music Festival, advertising a performance of Verdi's *I Vespri Siciliani*, an opera we had never heard before. The poster announced that Erich Kleiber was to conduct and the great Bulgarian basso, Boris Christoff, was to be a member of the cast, and we had to get tickets and go. The performance started at 9 p.m. (it was over at about 1:30 a.m.), and we had "seats" in the upper reaches of the balcony, which meant sitting on stone steps as in an amphitheater. Never mind the physical discomfort (Mimi was newly pregnant;) we were young and in musical heaven.

During the first act, out came a hefty woman who sang divinely — literally, as though an angel had emerged from the wings. I looked at the program and found I had never heard of the artist. Her

FIDELIO

Oper in zwei Akten von
LUDWIG VAN BEETHOVEN

Dirigent: Wilhelm Furtwängler
Inszenierung: Günther Rennert
Bühnenbild und Kostüme: Emil Preetorius
Orchester: Die Wiener Philharmoniker
Chor der Wiener Staatsoper

Florestan, ein Gefangener	Julius Patzak
Leonore, seine Gemahlin (Fidelio)	Kirsten Flagstad
Don Fernando, Minister	Hans Braun
Don Pizarro, Kommandant eines Staats-gefängnisses	Paul Schöffler
Rocco, Kerkermeister	Josef Greindl
Marzelline, seine Tochter	Elisabeth Schwarzkopf
Jacquino, Pförtner	Anton Dermota
Erster Gefangener	Hermann Gallos
Zweiter Gefangener	Ljubomir Pantscheff

Staatsgefangene, Wachen, Volk

Ort und Zeit: Spanien zur Zeit Karls III. um 1770

Nach dem zweiten Bild eine größere Pause

3

Program of the 1950 Salzburg Festival performance of Fidelio *conducted by Wilhelm Furtwängler, starring Kirsten Flagstad and Elisabeth Schwarzkopf (Wolf Trap Collection).*

DON GIOVANNI

Dramma Giocosa in due atti
dell'Abate Lorenzo da Ponte

Musik von
W. A. MOZART

Dirigent: Wilhelm Furtwängler

Inszenierung: Oscar Fritz Schuh

Choreographie: Erika Hanka

Bühnenbild: Clemens Holzmeister

Kostüme: Caspar Neher

Orchester: Die Wiener Philharmoniker

Chor und Ballett der Wiener Staatsoper

Don Giovanni . . . . Tito Gobbi
Donna Elvira . . . . Elisabeth Schwarzkopf
Der Gouverneur . . . . Josef Greindl
Donna Anna, dessen Tochter . . . . . Ljuba Welitsch
Don Ottavio, ihr Bräutigam . . . . . Anton Dermota
Leporello . . . . Erich Kunz
Zerline, ein Bauernmädchen . . . . . Irmgard Seefried
Masetto, Zerlinens Bräutigam . . . . Alfred Poell

Nach dem ersten Aufzug eine größere Pause

*

IN ITALIENISCHER SPRACHE

3

Program of the 1950 Salzburg Festival performance of Don Giovanni *conducted by Wilhelm Furtwängler, with Tito Gobbi, Elisabeth Schwarzkopf, Ljuba Welitsch, and Irmgard Seefried (Wolf Trap Collection).*

PERSONAGGI   INTERPRETI

Guido di Monforte   .   .   .   .   . Enzo MASCHERINI
Il Sire di Bethune   .   .   .   .   .   Bruno CARMASSI
Il Conte Vaudemont   .   .   .   .   .   . Mario FROSINI
Arrigo .   .   .   .   .   . Giorgio KOKOLIOS-BARDI
Giovanni da Procida .   .   .   .   . Boris CHRISTOFF
La Duchessa Elena   .   .   . Maria MENEGHINI-CALLAS
Ninetta   .   .   .   . Mafalda MASINI
Danieli   .   .   .   . Gino SARRI
Tebaldo   .   .   .   . Aldo DE PAOLI
Roberto   .   .   .   . Lido PETTINI
Manfredo .   .   .   . Brenno RISTORI

Nobili, Siciliani, Siciliane, Soldati francesi

Danze composte da
AURELIO M. MILLOSS e JUREK SHABELEWSKI

Atto II - "Tarantella,, - eseguita da
Vanna BUSOLINI - Marcella OTTINELLI - Jolanda RAPALLO
e il Corpo di Ballo femminile

Atto III - "Il Ballo delle Stagioni,, - eseguito da
Jacqueline MOREAU   .   .   .   .   . La Prima Ballerina
Wladimir SKOURATOFF   .   .   . Il Principe d'Autunno
Violette VERDY)
Deryk MENDEL   (.   .   .   .   . Spiriti dell'Inverno
Marc BEAUDET   )
Wladimir OUKHTOMSKY   .   .   . Il Principe della Primavera
Xenia PALLEY   .   .   .   .   .   .   La Dama dell'Estate
Filippo MORUCCI .   .   .   . Il Fauno
Tatiana OUSPENSKA, Jolanda RAPALLO .   .   .   . Baccanti
Michèle ANDREN, Annemarie CORALLI, Jolanda RAPALLO
Roland CAZENAVE, Alberto MORO, Kiryl VASSILKOWSKY
(Pastorelle e Pastori)
Il Corpo di Ballo (I gruppi delle varie Stagioni)

Orchestra, Coro e Corpo di Ballo del Maggio Musicale Fiorentino

Maestro concertatore e direttore
ERICH KLEIBER

Maestro direttore del Coro
ANDREA MOROSINI

Program of 1951 Florence May Music Festival: I Vespri Siciliani *with Maria Callas and Boris Christoff, and conducted by Erich Kleiber (Wolf Trap Collection).*

name was Maria Menegheni Callas. (Frankly, I never heard her sing as well again, and I admit that in later years I became a critic of her voice, if not of her stage characterizations. Her inattention to pitch, her occasional broad and undisciplined vibrato, and her excessive scooping to reach high notes spoiled a number of her later performances for me.) But that *I Vespri* was unforgettable.

One other aspect of that performance was also unforgettable: when the tenor—who shall remain nameless here—appeared on stage for the first time, the audience immediately began to boo, even before he began to sing. The booing persisted until the tenor left the stage without having sung a note. Every time he subsequently appeared on the stage, the booing would begin again and continue until he disappeared. He never sang a note in the entire performance—an *I Vespri* without its tragic tenor!

A frequent visitor to our musical offerings at the America House was an elderly, well-dressed gentleman who eventually introduced himself as Walther Kirchhoff, a retired opera singer who lived in Frankfurt. The name rang a bell, but only after questioning him further did I learn that he had been a leading Wagnerian tenor at the Metropolitan Opera, starting in 1926 and continuing to sing there successfully until 1932.

As we became acquainted, he told me that he had made his debut in Berlin in 1906, some forty-five years earlier. Years later, I looked him up in Irving Kolodin's book, *The Metropolitan Opera, 1883–1966*,[3] which described his debut as Loge in *Rheingold* as "one of the finest impersonations of the subtle and crafty schemer New York had seen." He sang all the leading Wagnerian roles, and eventually none other than Loritz Melchior succeeded him. Kirchhoff was a pleasant and modest gentleman, eager to talk about his operatic exploits and apparently delighted to find an equally eager listener.

The Boston Symphony Tour

In 1952 I was asked to serve as the State Department escort for the Boston Symphony tour in Germany, its first postwar visit in that country. For me this was an unexpected honor and a wonderful opportunity to be involved with one of the great orchestras of the world. On the tour, the orchestra was alternatingly conducted by Charles Munch, then its music director, and Pierre Monteux, its earlier music director. I picked up the orchestra in Brussels, where Munch conducted, and escorted them first to Frankfurt and then to Berlin.

The author escorting the conductor Pierre Monteux to the concert of the Boston Symphony in Frankfurt, 1952 (U.S. Information Service).

Monteux conducted both of those concerts, and I was able to get to know that venerable maestro, however briefly. Delightful and most cooperative to work with, he acted as though he were too old and infirm to climb onto the podium; but once he made it, he conducted with the enthusiasm and energy of a young man. His motions with his long baton were measured, but his eyes sparkled as he cued his musicians with an encouraging glance. A superb conductor!

In Frankfurt Monteux conducted Brahms' Third Symphony and William Schuman's Third Symphony, along with some Berlioz, Ravel, and Richard Strauss. In Berlin the orchestra also played Hindemith's *Mathis der Maler*.

As escort I had really only one problem: the orchestra traveled from Frankfurt to Berlin in a sealed military train through the Soviet Zone of Germany. It was the only available mode of travel, as it was not practical to transport the whole orchestra and instruments on the limited PanAm flights between the two cities. Most members of the orchestra were completely at ease with the arrangement and even considered it an adventure, but some, mostly former refugees from the Soviet Union and Eastern Europe, were apprehensive and required calming down and hand-holding before they agreed to make the trip. All went well, and the orchestra, as usual, played magnificently.

Several weeks later I received a thank-you letter from George Judd, the orchestra's longtime manager, in which he offered assistance if I were interested in joining the orchestra's administration. I was tempted, but I declined with regret, figuring that I wanted to continue in my budding diplomatic career.

The Solti Connection

Georg Solti came to Frankfurt in 1952 as the newly appointed music director (*Generalmusikdirektor*) of the Frankfurt Opera and of the *Museumsorchester* (the Frankfurt Philharmonic). His arrival nearly coincided with the inauguration of a new opera house, which replaced a makeshift hall in the Frankfurt stock exchange where the opera company had performed since the end of World War II. (The grandiose old opera house was a conspicuous ruin near the center of the city and was rebuilt as a concert hall only in the 1980s.)

Solti's reputation as a fine conductor preceded him, and almost immediately both the orchestras under his direction and the opera artists benefited from his ability to build an ensemble opera and create productions that were exciting, musically of a high caliber, and superbly executed. He did not have singers of great reputation in his company but succeeded with an assembly of mostly young artists, eager to follow his leadership.

We met early in his tenure on a less than auspicious occasion. The U.S. consulate general had denied him a visa to travel to the United States at the invitation of the Chicago Symphony to conduct concerts at the Ravinia Festival in the summer of 1952. The reason he was given for the refusal was that he had ostensibly had Communist connections in Munich, where he had been music director of the opera before coming to Frankfurt. He asked me, as the U.S. cultural affairs officer at the Consulate General, whether I could help clear up the problem. (I should interject here that Solti's own recall of this episode, as recorded in his *Memoirs*,[4] is somewhat different from my memory of the affair.)

I remember telling him that if he could give me his word that he had never had any Communist associations, I would try to help him clear up this serious problem. He assured me that he had never had anything to do with Communists or communism in Munich or elsewhere. I appealed to the visa officer in charge of the case, Tom Butler, but he refused to budge, as was his privilege. I solicited the assistance of a consulate colleague and friend, Howard Rohde, and with the approval of the consul general an investigation was launched by the Army's CIC unit that had produced the initial accusation.

One should remember that all this transpired at the time of Senator Joseph McCarthy's attacks against the State Department for its alleged Communist subversion, and many people, colleagues included, were afraid to question the accuracy of any accusation of Communist association. (I had my own run-in with two of Senator McCarthy's "junketeering gumshoes," Roy Cohn and David Shine, at the Frankfurt America House during Easter weekend 1953 and came out unscathed only because their investigation found that I had been a member of only two organizations during my short lifetime, the Boy Scouts of America and the U.S. Army.)[5]

It took several months before the mistake was acknowledged and cleared up. There had been a U.S. Army intelligence raid of a Communist cell in Munich, and, as Solti correctly writes in his memoirs, two lists were found—one of people who cooperated with the Communists and one of those who refused. Solti's name appeared on the second list, but the two lists had been erroneously amalgamated and he had thus been tainted.

At any rate, Solti missed his first invitation to Chicago, and it was only two years later that he was able to conduct that venerable orchestra at Ravinia. When he and his wife, Hedi, returned from that trip, we met them at the airport. The first thing I remember

Georg Solti in our Frankfurt apartment in 1953 studying the score of Verdi's Un Ballo in Maschera *while listening to a Toscanini recording of the opera (H. N. Tuch).*

Solti saying on greeting Mimi and me—we were by that time on a first name basis, Gyuri and Tom—was, "Tom, someday that orchestra is going to be mine." He mentioned later that he had been concerned because the orchestra had scheduled only two rehearsals for a concert that included Bartok's difficult *Concerto for Orchestra*. But, he added, "Not to worry: *they practice!*"

The two couples—Gyuri, Hedi, Mimi, and I—were often together, sometimes after performances in a restaurant, usually with other people from the opera company, including Solti's nominal boss, Harry Buckwitz, and his wife. Buckwitz was the general director (*Intendant*) of the Frankfurt Opera and Theater, the man who brought Solti to Frankfurt, and his close friend. At other times the Soltis and the Tuchs went on weekend excursions, to eat at a good restaurant in the country, and once, to drive down to Darmstadt to hear Inge Borkh sing Salome at the local opera, preparatory to her singing the same role in Frankfurt.

I remember Hedi and Gyuri coming to our apartment one Sunday afternoon while he was preparing a new production of Verdi's *Un Ballo en mascara*. I happened to have had a huge commercial playback machine (borrowed from the U.S. Army) and a noncommercial recording of Toscanini's *Ballo* with the NBC Orchestra which Gyuri was anxious to hear. We spent the afternoon listening and relistening to the recording, while Gyuri sat with his nose in his score.

Gyuri was invited to conduct *Don Giovanni* at the Glyndebourne Festival in 1954, and we decided to go together, to have a brief vacation. But since our daughter Andy had been born in March, and Mimi was nursing the baby, I accompanied the Soltis for a week without her. I stayed in a hotel in nearby Hove (next to Brighton), while they were "invited"—required—to stay in the Christie mansion on the grounds of the Glyndebourne estate.

We had agreed that on the first morning after our arrival I would take a bus over to Glyndebourne, and we would spend the day together. Early that morning I received a call from Gyuri who announced, "Change of plans. We will drive over and pick *you* up." They arrived about an hour later, and Gyuri immediately wanted to see my room. I demurred that it had not yet been made up, but he insisted. So Hedi, he, and I went up to the room; he immediately headed for the bathroom, whence he emerged and announced, "Hedi, we will come here every morning to take our baths—with Tom's permission, of course." Then he turned to me and explained, "In the mansion we have to share a bath with Vittorio Gui [the conductor] and he leaves hair in the bathtub!" And so they did for the entire week.

Solti conducted a wonderful *Don Giovanni* in the small intimate Glyndebourne theater. His Don was James Pease, Leporello was Benno Kusche, the three ladies were Margaret Harshaw, Sena Jurinac (one of my all-time favorite singers), and Anni Schlemm, a young soprano and Solti protégé whom he had brought from Frankfurt. Leopold Simoneau sang the finest Don Ottavio I have ever heard.

Glyndebourne itself is an experience I will treasure for a long time. Most of the ticket holders came from London by special train, dressed in black tie and formal evening gowns, carrying picnic baskets and bottles of wine. Performances at that time started at 5 p.m. During the main intermission, which lasted one to two hours, spectators spread blankets on the lawn and enjoyed their repast al fresco, strolling around the lovely garden after supper, before returning to the theater for the remainder of the performance. Afterwards they would climb back on the train for their trip back to London. Hedi, Gyuri and I had our meals in a large tent reserved for the artists and staff of the opera company.

In the Original Italian

DON GIOVANNI

Ossia

Il dissoluto Punito

Opera in due Atti

Poesia di Lorenzo da Ponte   Musica di W. A. Mozart

Leporello, *Servant to Don Giovanni*   ..   ..   Benno Kusche (*German*)
Donna Anna, *Daughter of the Commendatore and*
   betrothed to Don Ottavio   ..   ..   Margaret Harshaw (*American*)
Don Giovanni, *a Young and Licentious Nobleman*   James Pease (*American*)
The Commendatore   ..   ..   Hervey Alan (*English*)
Don Ottavio   ..   ..   Léopold Simoneau (*Canadian*)
Donna Elvira, *a Lady from Burgos,*
   abandoned by Don Giovanni   ..   ..   Sena Jurinac (*Bosnian*)
Zerlina, *a Peasant Girl*   ..   ..   ..   Anny Schlemm (*German*)
Masetto, *a Peasant, betrothed to Zerlina* ..   .. Thomas Hemsley (*English*)

Conductor: GEORG SOLTI   Producer: CARL EBERT

Designer: JOHN PIPER

THE ROYAL PHILHARMONIC ORCHESTRA

Continuo played by the Conductor

THE GLYNDEBOURNE FESTIVAL CHORUS AND BALLET

Scenery built by THE RINGMER BUILDING WORKS LTD. *under the supervision of* R. W. GOUGH
and S. ZEAL
Scenery painted at THE AMBASSADORS SCENIC STUDIOS *under the supervision of* CHARLES BRAVERY
Costumes made by THE GLYNDEBOURNE OPERA WARDROBE *under the supervision of* ROSEMARY VERCOE
Wigs by WIG CREATIONS   *Shoes by* GAMBA
Properties and Decorations made at GLYNDEBOURNE *under the supervision of* HARRY KELLARD

DATES OF PERFORMANCE: July 7 · 9 · 11 · 14 · 17 · 21 · 23 · 25 · 27

Program page of the 1954 Glyndebourne Festival production of Don
Giovanni, *conducted by Georg Solti with James Pease, Margaret Harshaw,
Sena Jurinac, and Leopold Simoneau (Wolf Trap Collection).*

I witnessed three other productions at Glyndebourne during that week: Stravinsky's *Rake's Progress*, conducted by Paul Sacher; Richard Strauss's *Ariadne auf Naxos*, conducted by John Pritchard, with Sena Jurinac, the American coloratura soprano Mattiwilda Dobbs, and Lucine Amara singing the three leading female roles; and Rossini's *Cenerentola*, also conducted by John Pritchard, with the Spanish mezzo soprano, Maria de Gabarin, Juan Oncina, and Sesto Bruscantini. Performances at Glyndebourne were at the time—and, I am sure, still are—exceptional musical experiences, and for the London commuters, I imagine, classy affairs.

Solti created many outstanding musical performances in Frankfurt. He produced several contemporary works: Hindemith's *Cardillac*, Rolf Liebermann's *Penelope*, and Stravinsky's *Oedipus Rex*, *Mavra*, and *Le Renard*; and he created new productions of his inaugural opera *Carmen*, *Salome*, *Otello*, *Cosi Fan Tutte*, *Don Giovanni*, *Magic Flute*, *Un Ballo en Mascara*, and *Rosenkavalier*.

With the Museumsorchester, Gyuri conducted several memorable concerts, among them Beethoven's Ninth and *Missa Solemnis*, Brahms's *Ein Deutsches Requiem*, and concerts with the pianist Wilhelm Backhaus (Beethoven's Piano Concerto no. 3), with the pianist Edwin Fischer (Beethoven's Piano Concerto no. 5), and with the baritone Dietrich Fischer-Dieskau (Mahler's *Das Lied von der Erde*).

We left Frankfurt in March 1955, and, to our regret, we saw and heard Georg Solti only intermittently during the following years, whenever and wherever our paths would cross. When he and Hedi divorced, we were shocked, but by then the four of us had been separated by geography and circumstances, certainly not through either party's fault. The last time we met Gyuri was in Frankfurt in 1985, when he conducted the Chicago Symphony in the Ninth Symphony of both Bruckner and Shostakovich.

I am the first to recognize that musically I was greatly influenced by Georg Solti. I learned a lot from him, not in any technical sense—after all I was a mere aficionado—but aesthetically and emotionally. Through my association with him I became convinced that it was the conductor who, by guiding, shaping, and controlling everything on the stage and in the pit, made an opera performance successful, and thus I often remember a performance—for better or for worse—not so much by who sang or who directed but by who conducted it.

Other Memorable Musical Moments

Until the end of the 1950s, opera performances in Germany were usually sung in German, as operas in other European countries were also sung in the vernacular. Thus I learned opera stories and texts initially not in the opera's original language but in German translation. It was not until the early 1960s that opera stars began the practice of jetting from one country's opera house to another on a regular basis. The internationalization of opera companies became a reality and operas in European houses began to be sung regularly in the composition's original language.

In the United States, the Metropolitan Opera and other principal opera companies usually produced their operas in the original language, and it was rare to have a standard work sung in English, one such rarity being the Met's *Cosi fan tutte* in 1952 under Fritz Stiedry, with Richard Tucker, Eleanor Steber, and Blanche Thebom. (Solti, when hearing a recording of this production in our apartment, complained that Blanche Thebom sang flat throughout the performance. "How can such a thing happen?" he asked.) American singers, well-trained in American conservatories and conversant in an opera's original language, became popular and much in demand in European opera houses in the 1960s, a topic I shall return to later. At this point, however, I recount some musical experiences in the 1950s that stand out in my memory. The most vivid of these undoubtedly is our visit to the 1953 Pablo Casals Music Festival in Prades near the French border with Spain.

Mimi and I and our friends, Dorothyann (DA) and Howard Rohde, set out on a vacation trip through France with the Pablo Casals Festival in Prades as our musical goal. From Frankfurt we hit some of the touristic and culinary high spots in central France: the Loire valley, Orleans, Tours, Poitiers, Limoges, Perigeux, the Lascaux caves, Carcassonne, Perpignan, and finally Prades at the foot of the Pyrenees. We found pleasant accommodations in nearby Argeles-sur-Mer on the Costa Brava since Prades itself was too small a town to house all the music lovers attending the festival.

Performances that year took place in the Abbey of St. Michel de Cuxa, situated a half mile from the town up a steep dirt road. Artists and tourists trudged up to the church mostly on foot. I remember picking up Madeline Foley, lugging her cello, and Karen Tuttle her viola as they hitchhiked up to the church. (Madeline played her cello in the orchestra sitting next to Paul Tortelier, and Karen sat next to the principal violist, Joseph de Pasquale, on vacation from the Boston Symphony.) It was all quite informal, and the atmosphere

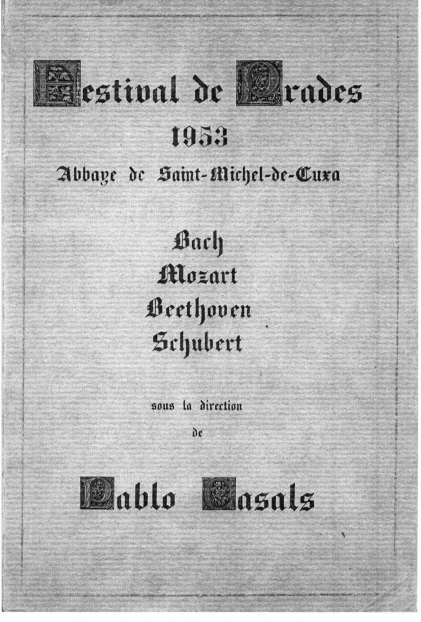

Program booklet of the Casals Music Festival in Prades, France, 1953 (Wolf Trap Collection).

in the packed church was one of intimacy and communion with the artists on the stage.

Pablo Casals certainly occupied the center of that stage. He conducted the orchestra (which in itself constituted an amalgam of famed instrumental soloists, among them the flutist John Wummer of the New York Philharmonic, the oboist Marcel Tabuteau of the Philadephia Orchestra, and Jacob Krachmalnik, the concertmaster of the Prades orchestra and of the Philadelphia Orchestra). One orchestral program consisted of the Bach Brandenburg Concerto no. 5, with Rudolph Serkin playing the piano, Krachmalnik the solo violin, and John Wummer the solo flute. That same concert also included the Beethoven Piano Concerto no. 2, with Rudolph Serkin, and a Mozart violin concerto, with Joseph Fuchs as soloist.

Casals also played his cello in chamber music concerts with Serkin, Lillian and Joseph Fuchs, and by himself. Another chamber music concert featured Maria Stader and the pianist William Kappell (shortly before the latter's untimely death in an airplane crash) in a performance of a heart-stopping Mozart's *Exultate Jubilate*. This was indeed unforgettable music making.

On our return trip we "did" Arles, Nîmes, and Avignon, ending our travels in France in the little town of Vienne, near Lyons. Why Vienne? Vienne boasted a Roman temple and amphitheater, but its fame rested on the presence in that town of the Restaurant de la Pyramide, and we had come to worship at the altar of its famous chef, Fernand Point, recognized in all of France as the proprietor of the number one of all the three-star restaurants.

We had planned our last stop in Vienne from the beginning of our trip, and we had budgeted for this last expenditure, hoarding the extravagant sum of $9.00 (2500 francs) per person that we knew in advance was going to be the cost (minus wine) of our dinner. What Prades was to music, M. Point's kitchen was to culinary art — pure bliss!

American Ballet Theater in Frankfurt

In the fall of 1953 I was asked by the State Department to help look after the American Ballet Theater (ABT) during its three-day stop in Frankfurt as an official U.S. performing arts presentation. Although this was not an opera or concert performance, it was a noteworthy event, exemplifying the type of presentation that was part of the U.S. government's cultural diplomacy at that time.

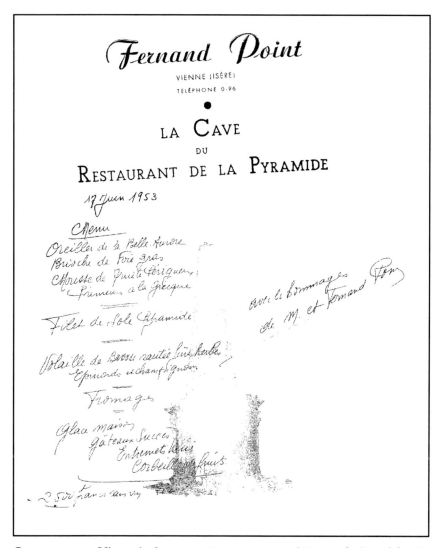

Our menu at Vienne's 3-star restaurant, as written and signed by its world famous owner-chef, Fernand Point.

The ABT's program in Frankfurt consisted of *Les Sylphides*, Agnes de Mille's *Harvest According*, the Black Swan pas-de-deux from *Swan Lake* (featuring the ABT's stars Alicia Alonso and Igor Youskevich), and the Jerome Robbins and Leonard Bernstein *Fancy Free*. It presented several ballet luminaries, among them Ruthann Koesun, John Kriza, Melissa Hayden, Eric Braun, and Mary Ellen Moylan. For the Frankfurt audiences this was a genuine revelation, the first appearance of this major American ballet company there.

A second reason for writing about this event is that I became more personally involved with the company than I would have wished. On the day after their arrival, the Frankfurt police called to inform me that they had arrested a member of the company for exposing himself in a park and behaving indecently. At the police station I learned that the culprit was the staff pianist, a British subject, whom the company had engaged during an earlier stop in London and brought along to the continent for their European appearances.

I happened to have been acquainted with the chief of police, and we were able to arrange that I would pick up the prisoner every evening on my recognizance, take him to the theater for the performance, and return him to the pokey afterwards. All went well until the last evening: The pianist was required to play in the last ballet on the program, *Fancy Free*, which has an important solo piano part. I was standing backstage watching the ballet when the moment came, near the beginning, for the piano to come in alone and play a short rhythmic ditty. No sound came from the orchestra except a soft humming of the piano tune by the conductor, so as to cue the dancers on the stage who continued to dance as though nothing was awry. I looked down in the pit and saw that the pianist's stool was empty.

I immediately suspected that my prisoner had flown the coop, and I saw myself already in his place in chains. I rushed around looking for him and fortunately found him in the orchestra's dressing room, lying on a bench, asleep. I woke him rudely, pushed him back to the stage to finish his job. As I yelled at him, he came up with the excuse that his experience in prison had been exhausting and that he needed to take a nap. After the performance I drove him back to jail and told the jailer to keep him until he rotted. The company had to find a replacement pianist.

The audience, I was told, did not notice what had happened; the artists had continued to dance to the conductor's humming. As for me, I chalked up the event to experience, but could not resist recording it here for posterity.

Präsident Blevins Davis

zeigt

THE AMERICAN NATIONAL

Ballet Theatre

Direktion: LUCIA CHASE und OLIVER SMITH

ALICIA ALONSO   IGOR YOUSKEVITCH   JOHN KRIZA

MARY ELLEN MOYLAN   MELISSA HAYDEN

Ruth Ann Koesun   Eric Braun

Lillian Lanese	Michael Lland	Jenny Workman	Kelly Brown
Dorothy Scott	Liane Plane	Barbara Lloyd	Scott Douglas
Fernaud Nault	Enrique Martinez	Vernon Lusby	Lila Popper
Irma Grant	Catherine Horn	Erik Kristen	Christine Mayer
Isabel Mirrow	Robert Haulin	Rochelle Balze	William Burdick
Vernon Wendorf	Margaret Watson	Donald Spottswood	Eugene Tanner
Nancy Unger	Sally Gura	Marilynn Oden	Ivan Allen
Helen Murielle	Leo Duggan	Yvonne Oudry	Howard Jeffrey
	Nansi Clement	Deborah Lovering	

Musikalische Leitung
JOSEPH LEVINE

Regisseur	*Dirizent*	*Balletmeister*
DIMITRI ROMANOFF	PAUL STRAUSS	EDWARD CATON

Es spielt das Orchester der Städtischen Bühnen

Alleiniger Manager für Europa
ANATOLE HELLER Bureau Artistique International / 15. rue La Boetie, Paris 8e

New York Office THE BALLET THEATRE, 152 West 56th Street, New York

Program page of the American National Ballet Theatre in Frankfurt (Wolf Trap Collection).

Les Sylphides *(H. N. Tuch).*

Alicia Alonso and Igor Youskevitch dancing the Pas de Deux the "Black Swan" from Swan Lake *(H. N. Tuch).*

Bayreuth—1954

In the summer of 1954 I had my one and only Bayreuth experience. Mimi declined to go, so a friend, Frank Gurley, and I took off for the drive to Bayreuth, arriving there barely in time to check into our hotel before the starting time of the performance, 5 p.m. The opera was *Parsifal*, my first hearing of this seminal Wagner opera.

As we were seated and the lengthy prelude had commenced, the long, tiring drive caught up with me, and I dozed off. A tap on my shoulder awakened me, and a voice whispered from the row behind me, "You can't go to sleep until the curtain goes up." I turned around and saw a friend wagging a finger at me. It was Patricia Connor, a young American soprano, who had given recitals and short performances (such as Menotti's *The Telephone*) at the America House, together with a young German baritone, Hans Neugebauer, who, years later became a Régisseur (director) at the Cologne Opera. I had not noticed Pat sitting behind me, but that "wake-up call" has stuck in my mind to this day.

The performance was great, both musically and dramatically. Wieland Wagner was the director in what was described as one of his most emotionally convincing productions. Hans Knappersbusch was the conductor, pacing the production very deliberately but creating a fine overall effect. Wolfgang Windgassen was Parsifal, Martha Mödl sang Kundry, Josef Greindl sang Gurnemanz, Hans Hotter was Amfortas, Gustav Neidlinger was Klingsor, and Ludwig Weber sang Titurel.

Keeping to the principle of full disclosure, I am not a Wagnerian in its usually exaggerated sense. I love much of his music and am enthralled hearing most of several of his operas. But I have always felt that, like many good authors, Wagner would have benefited from a good editor. (That's why I like Lorin Maazel's recording, *The "Ring" Without Words*, with the Berlin Philharmonic—59 minutes and 38 seconds in all.) Admittedly, any editor would have had a tough time with Wagner, who allegedly wrote his story backward and needed all those reprises to keep the story straight in his own mind. (So whatever happened to Alberich?)

I do greatly admire *Die Meistersinger*—with a few cuts—and *Tristan and Isolde*—minus Tristan's eternal ravings at the beginning of the last act. So let this be a confession with a plea for absolution from those of my friends who find no greater venal sin than casting aspersions on "Richard the Great."

BAYREUTHER FESTSPIELE

SAMSTAG 21. AUGUST 1954

PARSIFAL EIN BÜHNENWEIH-

FESTSPIEL VON RICHARD WAGNER

AMFORTAS: HANS HOTTER · TITUREL: JOSEF GREINDL · GUR-
NEMANZ: LUDWIG WEBER · PARSIFAL: WOLFGANG WIND-
GASSEN · KLINGSOR: GUSTAV NEIDLINGER · KUNDRY:
MARTHA MÖDL · 1. GRALSRITTER: GENE TOBIN · 2. GRALS-
RITTER: THEO ADAM · 1. KNAPPE: HETTY PLÜMACHER
2. KNAPPE: GISELA LITZ · 3. KNAPPE: GERHARD STOLZE
4. KNAPPE: HUGO KRATZ · 1. BLUME I. GRUPPE: ILSE
HOLLWEG · 2. BLUME I. GRUPPE: FRIEDL PÖLTINGER
3. BLUME I. GRUPPE: HETTY PLÜMACHER · 1. BLUME
II. GRUPPE: DOROTHEA SIEBERT · 2. BLUME II. GRUPPE:
JUTTA VULPIUS · 3. BLUME II. GRUPPE: GISELA LITZ · ALT-
SOLO: HETTY PLÜMACHER · DIRIGENT: HANS KNAPPERTS-
BUSCH · REGIE UND INSZENIERUNG: WIELAND WAGNER
CHÖRE: WILHELM PITZ · CHOREOGRAPHIE: GERTRUD
WAGNER · MUSIKALISCHE EINSTUDIERUNG: MAXIMILIAN
KOJETINSKY · PAUL ZELTER · AUSSTATTUNGSLEITUNG:
OTTO WISSNER · BELEUCHTUNGS- UND TECHNISCHE BERA-
TUNG: PAUL EBERHARDT · BELEUCHTUNG: HANS RICHTER
ASSISTENZ: RUDOLF JOHN · MASKEN: WILLI KLOSE
TECHNISCHE BÜHNENLEITUNG: ARTHUR EISENSCHMIDT

Program of the 1954 performance of Parsifal *at the Bayreuth Festival;
Hans Knappertsbusch, conductor (Wolf Trap Collection).*

Thornton Wilder

One nonmusical but nonetheless outstandingly memorable experience came in the fall of 1954 with the visit of Thornton Wilder. Wilder had been invited to the Berlin Cultural Festival where his play *The Matchmaker* was going to be performed. He agreed to first spend a few days in Frankfurt to contribute to our America House cultural program. I met him at the airport upon arrival and took him to his hotel in town. I gave him his schedule of events and was about to leave when he stopped me and asked, "What's your wife's name?" I replied, "Mimi," and he said, "Why don't you call Mimi and ask her whether she would like to join us for lunch. You people constantly entertain visitors; let me return the favor and take you two out for a good meal." And so started a beautiful friendship the likes of which only a Thornton Wilder could generate.

He gave a lecture in the main auditorium of the Frankfurt University, which was so overcrowded that two adjoining lecture halls had to be opened and the speech piped in. Wilder's German was fairly fluent but somewhat ungrammatical. (He had had a German nanny, he told us.) Though reading from a text, he got carried away in his enthusiasm, waving his arms with pages of his manuscript in his hands, and suddenly he didn't know how to end a sentence. He looked down at his text, shuffled pages, couldn't find his place, finally looked up, and with barely a hesitation said, "*geworden sind,*" to an outburst of sympathetic laughter from his audience. (By way of an attempt at an inexplicable linguistic explanation: in German, sentences usually end with the all-important verb. By ending his sentence with a random verb, "have become," he followed German grammar rules correctly, simultaneously making absolutely no sense and spontaneous fun of German grammar.)

One evening we went to the theater together to see Georg Buechner's rarely performed *Dantons Tod* (*The Death of Danton*). It was a dreadful performance, with the actors trying to outshout each other, a near caricature of German acting. Thornton started whispering critical comments, which became risibly louder. I finally had to nudge him into silence to avoid embarrassment.

One reason he had made the trip to Germany was to look after the acclaimed actress Ruth Gordon, who played the title role in *The Matchmaker*. Ms Gordon, a good friend of Wilder's, was Jewish and had qualms about coming to Germany. She and her husband, Garson Kanin, the versatile theatrical guru, arrived in Berlin by air, and Thornton and I met them and kept them company during their stay in Berlin. Everything went very well—the play was a huge success and so were Ruth Gordon and, of course, Thornton Wilder.

After the premiere, Thornton suggested that we visit some of Berlin's drinking establishments, and we went bar-hopping until six in the morning. In one of Berlin's *Kneipen* (beer joints), we encountered Erich Kästner, the famous author of German children's books. (I grew up on his *Emil and the Detectives* and *Pünktchen und Anton*.) Kaestner greeted us as though we were lifelong friends, but he was totally inebriated, as, we were told, he was every night in this place.

The next morning I saw Thornton off, slightly overhung but still full of brio, on his return flight to the United States. As I said at the beginning of this tale, it was a lasting and memorable experience.

"Atoms for Peace" in Berlin

In the fall of 1954 I spent several weeks on special assignment in Berlin, managing a huge exhibition,"The Peaceful Uses of Nuclear Energy," in the American pavilion at the annual Berlin Industrial Fair. President Eisenhower's "Atomic Power for Peace" speech at the UN General Assembly in December 1953 had signaled a major U.S. foreign policy initiative. To implement this initiative, the newly established U.S. Information Agency (USIA) focused its resources on promoting the peaceful uses of nuclear energy throughout the world. The centerpiece of this effort became the large exhibition in Berlin, which attracted many thousands of visitors. After my stint managing this exhibit in Berlin, I was reassigned to Washington in March 1955 and spent the next fifteen months building similar "Atoms for Peace" exhibits in Japan, India, Pakistan, and Portugal. (My involvement with this subject also resulted in my first book, written with my close friend, Henry Dunlap, *Atoms At Your Service*, published by Harper & Brothers in 1957.)

The weeks in Berlin—without my family—allowed me plenty of time to familiarize myself with the opera and concert scene in that city. At that time Berlin was not yet divided by the Wall; but after the suppressed uprising in the Soviet Sector of Berlin in 1953, it had become a hot spot of the Cold War.

The focal point of my familiarization effort was the Städtische Oper (City Opera) in West Berlin. Its home had been totally bombed out, and it functioned in what had been a prewar operetta theater, also in West Berlin, near the Bahnhof Zoo. It was not to be rebuilt in its original location until 1961, when it was renamed Deutsche Oper. Under a series of distinguished directors, it competed for

The author saying goodbye to Thorton Wilder upon the latter's departure from Berlin in 1954 (U.S. Information Service).

preeminence in the Federal Republic with the opera houses in Munich, Frankfurt, Stuttgart, Hamburg, and Cologne.

In the 1950s the Städtische Oper commanded some first-rate vocal resources. It was run by one of the great European opera impresarios, Carl Ebert, who was also the director of the Glyndebourne Opera Festival in England. Fine singing performances appeared to be his first priority, with the conductor assuming a secondary role. Ebert himself functioned as the principal stage director.

It was there that I saw Verdi's *Nabucco* for the first time. Christel Goltz sang Abigail and Ernst Häfliger was Ismael. Christel Goltz was also the *Salome* in a production of the Strauss opera that further featured the by then legendary Margarete Klose as Herodias. A marvelous performance of Mozart's *Don Giovanni* included in the title role Dietrich Fischer-Dieskau, successor in the baritone dynasty of Heinrich Schlussnuss as both singer and actor. That performance further included the trio of ladies, Elisabeth Grümmer, Elfriede Trötschel, and Lisa Otto, as well as the noted tenor Helmut Krebs as Don Otavio. In Donizetti's *Don Pasquale,* Rita Streich was Norina, Krebs sang Ernesto, and Herbert Brauer was Don Malatesta. The latter, a fine lyric baritone, became a good friend. In opera he was somewhat in the shadow of Fischer-Dieskau, but his artistry and musicianship came to the fore whenever he appeared on the opera or recital stage.

I spoke about singers in Berlin but did not mention conductors. Advisedly so. There was an absence of first-rate and inspiring musical direction in the performances I witnessed. Lacking good conductors, even the superior singing talent—some of Europe's finest—was unable to create really memorable performances (with the exception of the outstanding Fischer-Dieskau and Grümmer). This was in conspicuous contrast with Frankfurt at that time, where Georg Solti had created a marvelous ensemble opera with good but not world-renowned singers and a repertory that was innovative and exciting.

I also attended a number of concerts by the great Berlin Philharmonic during my stay in Berlin. I want to mention two that stood out: one conducted by Hans Rosbaud featured Wolfgang Schneiderhan in the Brahms Violin Concerto, and the orchestra played Mahler's First Symphony; the other, conducted by Sergiu Celibidache, which featured the Brahms *German Requiem* with Elizabeth Grümmer and Dietrich Fischer-Dieskau as soloists.

Before the family's departure from Frankfurt in March 1955, I was able to visit Vienna briefly and while there heard a wonderful recital by Irmgard Seefried in the splendid Brahms Saal. Accompanied by

Erik Werba, she sang Lieder by Moussorsky, Wolf, Pfitzner, and Richard Strauss.

How Could You Serve in Germany?

I have been asked frequently, most often by Jewish friends in the United States, "How could you?" How could you, after your family was literally expelled from your native land, come back to Germany and work happily for so many years, first fostering the American-German rapprochment, and then promoting the continuing close partnership between the two countries?

I could certainly understand the question and the incredulity that accompanied it. Many of my Jewish friends had suffered expulsion from Germany in the course of one of the most vicious persecutions Western civilization had experienced. Some of their loved ones had perished in the Holocaust—parents, siblings, uncles, aunts, cousins, murdered through Nazi atrocity. It was a legitimate question that, frankly, I did not adequately consider until it had been posed so often.

The answer, however, was a simple one: I could not blame the young people in Germany with whom I interacted for what had gone on during the Nazi regime; I could not hold them responsible for the acts, the crimes, committed by their elders any more than I felt responsible for the injustices and misdeeds of the generation before mine. For me, it was impossible to make these young Germans— my generation—accept guilt and responsibility for what had gone on in their country when they were children.

As someone trained in history and committed to the improvement of international relations, I firmly believed that we must not ignore the past in the conduct of our current affairs. We could learn from the experience of previous generations to avoid, if possible, the mistakes of the past. I thus felt that in Germany I could contribute by making sure that the crimes—why, how, and by whom they were committed in the 1930s and 1940s—would be understood and remembered by the present generation and provide lessons for the future.

To be sure, I had not personally been emotionally or physically scarred as had those who lost relatives and friends in the Holocaust, and I accepted readily their inability and unwillingness to react in the same way I did. But that *was* my reaction and my rationale, and I have not changed my mind in the intervening years. Indeed, I have continued to engage enthusiastically in the process, a principal objective of U.S. foreign policy during that time, of forging a new relationship with a democratic Germany and assuring the endurance of our mutually beneficial partnership.

I should add that I have no doubt that had my father lived—he died in 1936 at age 46 of a brain tumor—my whole family would also have perished in the Holocaust. My father, a German veteran and prisoner of war in World War I, a bearer of the Iron Cross, considered himself a proud and loyal German and would not have believed that he would ever be considered otherwise by his government. I don't think he ever would have tried to leave his country until it was too late.

It was my realist and determined mother—his forty-year old widow— who arranged for my departure in October 1938, who hid six male relatives in her apartment during the *Kristallnacht* atrocities, and who managed her own departure for the Phillippine Islands as late as March 1940 before finally coming to the United States.

2

Washington and Munich 1955–1958

Washington

We spent the next two years in Washington, our first stateside assignment. We bought our first house in Wheaton, Maryland, then a suburb that at the time seemed quite distant from downtown. Three colleagues and I carpooled to our respective offices in the city. During the first year, spent building "Atoms for Peace" exhibits in various countries, I was on the road much of the time. The second year—a big change for me—I studied Russian intensively, in preparation for an assignment to Moscow.

In Washington in 1955, Mimi and I heard the Boston Symphony under Charles Munch, a pleasant reunion with members of the orchestra from Frankfurt and Berlin days. We also attended a recital by David Oistrakh, our first hearing of this great violinist, whom we would get to know during our subsequent tour of duty in Moscow.

En route to Japan on an official trip, I spent the night in San Francisco, where I heard the San Francisco Symphony under Enrique Jorda for the first time. On a short, official visit to New York, I attended a performance of Johann Strauss's *Die Fledermaus*, conducted by Julius Rudel at the New York City Opera. What made this performance memorable was the terrific debut of one Beverly Sills.

Russian language study, beginning in the summer of 1956, was the most intensive commitment to any academic discipline I have ever made. The course lasted eleven months, seven hours a day with different teachers of diverse backgrounds, and a minimum of two hours of home work. The ten students were not competing with one another, but none of us wanted to hold back progress of the class by not keeping up with the furious pace.

My family hardly saw me since, in addition to the Russian marathon, I was writing a book about the peaceful uses of nuclear energy. The result, however, made it all worthwhile: I spoke better Russian at the end of the eleven months than I subsequently did after three years in Moscow.

There was little time for music, and during 1956 I remember only two events worth mentioning here: one was another concert of the Boston Symphony, this time under Ernest Ansermet (Mozart no. 41, Debussy, Bartok, and Ravel); the second was a concert by the Berlin Philharmonic under Herbert von Karajan (Brahms no. 2, Cherubini, and Wagner). And on another business trip to New York, I heard *Rigoletto* at the old Met: Fausto Cleva conducted and the exemplary cast consisted of Richard Tucker, Robert Merrill, Hilde Gueden, Georgio Tozzi, and Sandra Warfield.

We were supposed to transfer to Moscow in the summer of 1957, but the Soviets kept delaying our visas, primarily, we learned later, because I was a USIA officer, belonging in Soviet eyes to that notorious "spy organization." I finally had to resign from USIA and be reappointed to the State Department before they would issue visas to the Tuch family. Threats of reciprocal visa denial to a Soviet diplomat assigned to Washington did the trick, and we transferred to Moscow in July 1958.

VOA in Munich 1957–1958

During the one-year wait for this to happen, we were transferred to Munich, where I served at the branch office of the Voice of America (VOA). My job was to write commentaries, to be a policy editor, and, on occasion, to serve as a correspondent.

VOA Munich had been established to broadcast in Russian, Ukranian, Uzbek, Polish, Hungarian, Romanian, Bulgarian, Lithuanian, Latvian, and Estonian to the respective countries in the Soviet Bloc, obtaining a better radio signal from Munich than could be accomplished from the distant United States.

Since VOA broadcast nearly twenty-four hours a day, seven days a week, I didn't have as much time to enjoy music as I would have liked in this music-rich city. Yet we did manage to hear some wonderful performances at the Bavarian State Opera, which operated in temporary facilities, the *Prinz-Regententheater*, pending the rebuilding of its former magnificent home.

Outstanding among the performances we heard was *Salome*, conducted by Josef Keilberth and featuring Inge Borkh in the title role; the *Marriage of Figaro*, conducted by Ferenc Fricsay and featurng Hermann Prey as Figaro; *Un Ballo in Mascara*, conducted by

Fricsay; and *Die Agyptische Helena* (*The Egyptian Helena*) by Richard Strauss, conducted by Keilberth, with Leonie Rysanek. The latter opera was an unannounced substitution for another opera we had come to hear; there were no programs with a synopsis of the story; the German was unintelligible, and frankly, we didn't know what was happening on the stage in this, our first hearing of the opera. We fared better with Strauss's *Die Frau Ohne Schatten*, also with the great Leonie Rysanek. Another first hearing was Carl Orff's *Der Mond* and *Die Kluge*, (*The Moon* and the *Wise One*).

On a quick business trip to Berlin, I heard Benjamin Britten's *Rape of Lucretia* in a performance notable because it was the first time I heard Thomas Stewart. And on a weekend trip to Vienna to see our close friends, Terry and Dottie Catherman, shortly before our departure for Moscow, we went to the Staatsoper to hear the *Magic Flute*, conducted by Borislav Klobucar with a stellar cast: Anton Dermota, Erich Kunz, Lisa della Casa, Mimi Coertse, Anneliese Rothenburger, and Ludwig Weber; and *Die Meistersinger von Nürnberg*, conducted by Josef Keilberth and featuring Gustav Neidlinger, Lisa della Casa, and Anton Dermota.

3

Moscow 1958–1961

To explain the context of our professional and musical activities in the late 1950s in Moscow, it is useful, I believe, to describe and discuss what it was like to live there as an American diplomatic family. I use the pronoun "we," since Mimi's role in our Moscow life was equal to mine and even more stressful, because I had an ever-interesting job to compensate for the hardships of existing in Moscow, while she had only the frustrations and difficulties of maintaining a family under the prevailing conditions.

We arrived in Moscow in July 1958 for what turned out to be a three-year tour of duty that resembeled a political rollercoaster. It started with "the spirit of Camp David," Chairman Nikita Khrushchev's visit to the United States in the summer of 1958, heralding the possibility of a gradual thawing of U.S.-Soviet relations. President Eisenhower was to reciprocate the visit, but the downing of Gary Power's U-2 spy plane on May 1, 1960, plunged the relationship to lower depths and the president's trip was abruptly cancelled.

Gradually, relations improved reciprocally with the election of President Kennedy in the fall of 1960, only to drop precipitously again with the Bay of Pigs invasion and to fall even lower during the disastrous Kennedy-Khruschev encounter in Vienna in July 1961.

Little of these atmospheric changes affected the lives of the families in the U.S. Embassy in their day-to-day existence. We were *the enemy*, and we were treated as such. Our apartments were bugged. (We did not even search for the bugs since they would immediately be replaced elsewhere if we found them.) We were "tailed" everywhere we went—not only embassy personnel but their spouses as well. This became so routine that our son David, then six years old, would look out the back window of our VW bug and yell, "Slow down, Daddy, you're losing your tail!"

Harassment would take many forms, some amusing, some annoying, some vicious. Our first encounter with the Soviet "system" came about when Mimi and I applied for driver's licenses. The Soviets had not wanted us to own cars and drive in Moscow, but Soviet diplomats in Washington enjoyed the freedom of their personal cars and had been notified that they were about to lose that privilege unless American diplomats in Moscow could drive their own vehicles while stationed there.

To obtain driver's licenses, we were forced to pass a tough exam that involved learning the Moscow traffic rules and regulations published in a sixty-page booklet. On our first try, we flunked— fair game, we thought. Then Mimi and I memorized the instruction booklet, in the process translating it into English for the benefit of our non-Russian-speaking embassy colleagues. At our second session, the Soviet examiners grilled us for forty minutes; they could not fault us on any question. (Example: Name the eight places in Moscow where you could not make a U-turn; name the nine corners in Moscow where you could not make a right turn.)

Both Mimi and I had the instruction booklet down pat. Finally the examiner asked me if my car were stuck on a railroad crossing, how far down the track did the crossing guard have to run to stop an oncoming train? I told him that the instruction book contained nothing about crossing guards' responsibilities. He knew that, he said, and advised me to buy the instruction book for railroad guards and memorize it as I had done the drivers' instruction book. Mimi got the same advice when she similarly could not answer a question about crossing guards' orders.

We stormed out furiously, frustrated by our first encounter with the Soviet harassment system. Back at the Embassy, I complained to our ambassador, Llewellyn "Tommy" Thompson. He calmly suggested that on my next visit to the Foreign Ministry I should enquire what second secretary in their Washington embassy should have his driver's license revoked. Two weeks later, at our third appointment with the license examiners, they asked us two simple questions each and handed us our licenses. Oh, that ever-effective principle of reciprocity!

We were tailed everywhere we drove in the city and outside Moscow (when we were given permission forty-eight hours ahead of time to drive beyond 25 kilometers from the city limits). Frequently, usually on a signal from our "tails," militiamen would stop us on the pretext that we had violated one rule or another. The most common was, in winter, the complaint that our Volkswagen was dirty. I would respond that the streets were full of slush that caused the car to be dirty. The policeman would announce that

"Socialist property has to be kept clean," and I would respond that our car was capitalist property. The policeman would give us a ticket. I would ostentatiously get out of the car, ask him for his badge number, and record the number of his license plate. I would tell him that I would report him to the Foreign Ministry for harassing a diplomat. I never heard anything further from the police, and he probably heard nothing from the Foreign Ministry.

At the time there were few foreign cars on the streets of Moscow. Wherever I stopped, the VW would immediately attract a number of inquisitive onlookers. "Where was this car made?" they would ask.

"In Germany."

"Your Germany or our Germany?"

"In the democratic Germany," I would answer, and I would show them the interior of the car. (In those days, the VW came equipped with a dipstick instead of a gas gauge.) When I opened the hood, I would exclaim in mock anger that someone had stolen my engine, then relax, open the rear compartment and tell them that fortunately this German car had a spare engine!

Initially, the embassy boasted an empathetic and practical staff physician, a young Air Force doctor who routinely made "preventive" house calls at odd hours, whenever he was in the neighborhood, checking on our childrens' possible colds and rashes. He also concocted huge batches of a combination of Kaopactate, Bismuth, and Bella Donna and bottled them as first aid medication for embassy officers to take with them on their travels around the country. While some of these ailments came about naturally, we also had repeated evidence that our diplomats were targeted for "bacterial attacks" while away from the capital on trips in the country.

Providing for the family's daily needs was a permanent challenge for Mimi. She stood in line daily, the winter cold notwithstanding, waiting for fresh bread to be delivered to the state store so that she could get some before the supply ran out and only yesterday's stale remainder was available. The collective and state farm markets yielded little that was edible during the winter months other than potatoes, onions, and the occasional carrot.

We had a miniscule commissary in the Embassy which was also made available to the small American press contingent (whom, at any rate, the Soviet authorities considered an adjunct of the embassy's "intelligence network"). When the first graduate students under the U.S.-Soviet Cultural Exchange Agreement arrived in the fall of 1958, we made an agreement with the students that they would stay away from contact with the embassy to emphasize their independent academic identification. It soon became evident, however, that the Soviets considered them also part of the "American spy network" (probably equating them with their Soviet "students" in the United States, some of whom were indeed identified as members of the Soviet security system), and so our students were happy to be included in the "American family," gathering from time to time in the commissary for purchases and gossip.

The principal source of goods for the embassy store was the U.S. Army commissary in Berlin, where we ordered supplies of frozen and canned goods. The system of transporting these foodstuffs was complicated: an embassy diplomat had to escort the shipment as his personal baggage from Warsaw to Moscow. Officers took turns traveling to Warsaw, meeting the train carrying the supplies from Berlin, and then accompanying the shipment back to the capital as their personal "luggage."

I was the chosen escort for such a shipment in October 1958. We arrived two hours late at Brest, the Polish-Soviet border. While the wheels of the passenger cars were automatically adjusted for the wider gauge of the Soviet railroad tracks, the freight cars had to be unloaded and reloaded in Soviet cars for the trip to Moscow. The conductor was not willing to wait while this was done and ordered the train to depart, leaving the freight cars behind in Brest. I argued with the conductor, telling him the nature of the shipment and claiming it was "diplomatic goods," etc., but to no avail. The train started moving, I jumped back on, leaving the shipment behind. I rode the rest of the way to Moscow wondering how I was going to explain my foul-up.

Imagine my welcome when the train arrived in Moscow and I reported the missing three-ton food shipment to the driver of the waiting embassy truck. What made it worse is that much of the frozen shipment was seafood and fish. When it became known that I was allergic to seafood and fish, it was immediately assumed that I had lost the shipment on purpose. I was in danger of becoming a "nonperson." Luckily for me, the weather in Brest had turned cold, and the missed shipment arrived the following morning still frozen solid. Yet, the sins one commits live after you: newly arrived officers who were about to be sent to accompany food shipments from Warsaw to Moscow were always warned about Tom Tuch's blunder.

We were encouraged by both the Department of State and Ambassador Thompson to travel within the Soviet Union in order to develop a wider perspective on the country than the capital provided. Such travel was difficult. Much of the Soviet Union was closed to travel by foreigners. (Reciprocally, we had closed parts of the United States to travel by Soviet diplomats.) Even the open areas were often "temporarily closed." Thus, when we applied the required two weeks in advance to visit, say, Tashkent, we would have to wait for permission before buying our airplane tickets, which, at the whim of the authorities, might or might not be available.

Again, if Soviet capriciousness became too obvious and annoying, the State Department invoked reciprocity. On one occasion we found that the entire country, even Leningrad, was "temporarily closed" to travel by U.S. diplomats. It so happened that the Soviet ambassador in Washington had an upcoming speaking engagement in Chicago. He was told that, unfortunately, Chicago had been temporarily closed to travel by the Soviet embassy. He evidently got the point, since the next day we were able to travel again, and he was able to deliver his speech in Chicago.

My first long trip in the fall of 1958 was to Uzbekistan, parts of which had just been opened to travel by U.S. diplomats. My steady travel companion-to-be—we always traveled in pairs— was my colleague and close friend, Ralph Jones. Ralph and I had previously served together in Munich. A widower with two young boys—the younger of whom, Philip, was our David's best friend—lived above us in our apartment complex. Ralph was a highly trained Russian expert, and he considered this assignment the apex of his career interests, to an even greater degree than I did. He was willing, at least at that point of his stay in the Soviet Union, to suffer the hardships of travel as part of his career experience, and was constantly admonishing me to do the same whenever my complaints became too vociferous.

We flew to Tashkent, where we were met by two female Intourist guides who, we understood immediately, were to be our "minders" during our stay. They indeed showed us around the city; but they tried to be more than guides, making all kinds of intimate suggestions, which we had anticipated. At first we were amused, then subsequently annoyed as their advances became cruder. We escaped their clutches by applying for travel to Bukhara, Samarkand, and Kokand. To our surprise, Bukhara and Samarkand were approved, and off we went to the former capitals of the "Golden Hordes."

Flying to Bukhara was an adventure in itself. We flew in an old Soviet knockoff of the C-47, the Li-2, which had no seats, only two benches along the bulkhead where two spaces were reserved for us. The rest of the passengers squatted on the floor. As the plane took off, the unattached benches and their occupants slid to the rear of the plane, causing apprehension as we tried to retain our balance.

Bukhara was fascinating. The city had not been bruised by World War II, and its many monuments, mosques, madrassas, government structures, and palaces—mostly in unadorned sandstone—were untouched but in disrepair, not yet restored for tourist-ready display. Samarkand was different: glorious in its multitude of colorful—mostly blue and gold tile—monuments, glistening in the the bright desert sun. It even had a small Intourist hotel, unlike Bukhara, where we had been accommodated in a building with a courtyard where a number of bunks were lined for tired travelers.

As we were flying back to Tashkent in our rickety aircraft, the co-pilot got up from his seat in the cockpit and examined an instrument hanging near the bulkhead. He motioned to the captain, who got up and joined him in examining the instrument, leaving the cockpit empty. I asked the captain, "*U vas avtomaticheski pilot?*"

"*Nyet,*" he replied, "this is a simple plane without automatic pilot." So much for safety regulations!

Back in Tashkent, in the hands of our two Intourist guides, we asked to see the opera *Ulugbek* by one A. Kozlovsky in the ornate opera house. At that, our escorts gave up on us in some disappointment and let us enjoy the only Uzbek opera that I am sure I will ever see. It is the story of the ancient Uzbek emperor (also identified in the West as Ulugh Beigh, after whom a crater on the moon is named) who became a great astronomer and mathematician under whose rule the thirteenth century empire thrived in scientific invention.

One other trip that Ralph and I took in the spring of 1959 was to Yerevan, the ancient capital of Armenia that had just been opened to travel by American diplomats. Upon arrival, several young men in their early twenties immediately approached us, speaking English, mostly with a distinct Brooklyn accent, obviously eager to have contact with us. We learned that they were Americans of Armenian descent whose families had been persuaded shortly after the end of World War II to be repatriated to their native Armenia. Although American citizens by birth, they were now stuck in Armenia, unable to get permission from the Armenian authorities to leave the country.

They were eager to talk with us, finding encouragement in having contact with Americans. We tried to impress upon them that it was dangerous for them to be seen with us, but they insisted that they didn't care: they just wanted to be with "their American friends." Ralph and I were saddened that we could do nothing at that time to encourage them in their predicament.

One of our objectives on this trip was to visit Echmeadzin, the "Vatican" of the ancient Armenian Catholic Church, and to call on the Catholicus, Vosgen I, the Armenian "pope." After considerable hesitation on the part of our "handlers" and our persistent insistence, the 45-minute drive was arranged. We were met at the monastery by an English-speaking Palestinian priest, who told us he would be our escort and interpreter (translation: "goon"). The first thing the Catholicus asked us when we were ushered into his reception chamber was whether we spoke any language other than Russian and English. We told him that we both spoke German. "Then let us have our conversation in German," he responded, with a wink at our escort. We had a pleasant, relaxed, and substantive talk for about forty-five minutes, during which we mentioned to him the plight of the young Americans we had met in Yerevan. Our escort-interpreter fidgeted in some discomfort, not understanding German and obviously worried about how he was going to report on our visit. The Catholicus, an outgoing Romanian by birth, presented us each with a souvenir, an engraved silver liqueur cup, after he had blessed it.

Long train trips were another way of trying to "communicate" with Soviet citizens in, so to speak, neutral territory. The "goons," who traveled with us but usually sat in an adjoining compartment, could hardly stop us from talking to the four or five fellow passengers who shared our compartment on lengthy train journeys to, say, Irkutsk, that took six to seven days. My "method" of starting conversations was by way of a Polaroid camera that I always carried with me. I initially snapped a photo of my traveling companion. That elicited immediate interest from fellow passengers, who asked to have their picture taken—and that usually started conversations, later developing into discussions that could last for days, beoming friendlier and more revealing as we shared cups of tea (prepared by the conductor), bottles of vodka, and food supplies that we had brought with us.

We had one highly unpleasant experience with train travel, however, that served as a caution to other colleagues. A newly arrived colleague, Kempton Jenkins, wanted to experience a lengthy train trip while we were visiting Kyrgyzstan in Central Asia. Against my better judgment, he suggested traveling from Frunze (now Bishtek) to Alma Ata (now Almati), the capital of Kazakhstan, by train. And so we did – to our regret! The train, when we boarded it, had been on the road for over a week, and the interior condition of the compartments, especially the odor, was not conducive to comfortable travel. We thus learned that, when planning a long trip, one should start in Moscow in a freshly cleaned and well-aired compartment.

A brief description of our living accommodations in Moscow might help clarify the context I cited at the beginning of this chapter, because these accommodations had a bearing on our ability to function as cultural representatives of our country. When we arrived in Moscow in the late summer of 1958, we were taken to a huge apartment complex on Prospekt Mira that had been constructed the previous year to house all foreign diplomats in Moscow. We had a roomy three-bedroom apartment; the kitchen and bathroom were equipped with U.S.-supplied appliances. Nets were hung over the sidewalk and building entrance from above the first floor to catch bricks that fell from the structure as the building "settled." We were repeatedly told not to worry—the falling bricks were a natural occurrence. Then one day, as we were having breakfast in our dining room, a tremendous crash emanated from our living room: the windows, glass and frames, had fallen out. Settlement indeed!

Suddenly, the authorities feared that the gas pipes might also crack, and the entire diplomatic corps were told to evacuate the complex immediately. Where were we to move? To accommodate us, the authorities evacuated a large apartment complex that had just been completed in a relatively new section of Moscow, Leninsky Prospekt. It had been built for worker families who, having just moved in, were peremptorily thrown out. The apartments were tiny two- and three-room dwellings with primitive appliances.

We were each assigned two adjoining apartments, one two-room and one three-room, necessitating going out into the hallway to go from one to the other. We managed to bring our American appliances from the old apartments to make our "temporary" abodes livable by our standards. I understand that today, almost fifty years later, American and other diplomatic families still occupy these make-do accomodations.

In one of its rare public interest exposures, *Vechernaya Moskva*, the evening newspaper, had been persuaded to publish the complaints of shoddy workmanship and lack of services in the new housing project by the Soviet occupants who had just been kicked out. Occupants, the paper reported, were warned not to step out onto the balconies since their weight might cause them to collapse. The occupants, the paper further wrote, were warned not to complain about the frequent lack of hot water, lest the supply be shut off completely!

Entertaining more than two or three visitors or other diplomats was nearly impossible because of lack of sitting space. Representative Wayne Hays of Ohio, a persistent critic of alleged luxuries and extravagant amenities for U.S. diplomats serving abroad, came to

Moscow in 1960 on one of his "inspection" visits. We invited him for lunch in our apartment(s), intending to show him how we lived. As he entered, he and his assistants were forced to duck under the wet bedding sheets that were hung in the hallway to dry. The hallway was lined with shelves on which we stored supplies that we had been permitted to ship in with our household goods—cans of orange and apple juice, cans of vegetables, chicken, and corned beef, coffee tins, cleaning supplies, toilet paper, and soap products. The congressman immediately appropriated a can of orange juice, claiming the hotel didn't serve it. The lunch that Mimi had prepared as best as she could didn't quite make the grade with Mr. Hays as he sat at the cramped table in our "dining room." The final intended reality check was planned for just before his departure: he asked to go the the bathroom. We did *not* tell him that the toilet, when flushed, would "spit" over the front, so it would be wise to step aside when applying the handle. A visibly embarrassed congressman departed in a hurry, covering his front with the purloined can of orange juice. To the best of my knowledge, our allowances were not cut that year.

Though the reader might demur, this lengthy digression from music and diplomacy seemed justified in a memoir of this kind, as I meant in these pages to explain the flavor of the "the life that late we led" (with apologies to Cole Porter).

Working as a U.S. Diplomat in Cold War Moscow

My assignment as press and cultural attaché in Moscow requires some background in why and how I became so involved with American and Soviet artists and performing arts groups. In January 1958, the United States and the Soviet Union signed a cultural agreement making possible exchanges of students, academics, creative artists, musicians, performing arts groups, exhibitions, and films on a reciprocal basis.[6]

Many bumps lay on the road to fulfilling the U.S. objectives of this agreement, which were, principally, to penetrate the Iron Curtain with information and cultural activities, reaching the maximum number of people in the Soviet Union to counter fifty years of misinformation and anti-American diatribes generated by the Soviet propaganda machine. We wanted in particular to promote a dialogue with the so-called "New Class" and with intellectuals, a traditionally privileged group in Russian society denied any contact with the West for a long time. We knew that the Soviets would try to resist this influx of information and restrict U.S. activities but would not, in the end, reject them entirely lest they fail to attain their own objectives in the agreement.

It was my principal assignment to look after U.S. interests in the agreement and to serve as embassy spokesman. Among the first delegations to come to the Soviet Union under the cultural agreement's auspices was a distinguished group of American composers—Roger Sessions, Roy Harris, Peter Mennin, and Ulysses Kay. Prevented from having any real contact with Soviet counterparts, they were instead herded from tedious discussions with Soviet cultural bureaucrats or cowed members of the Soviet Composers Union to endless rows of Soviet monuments with only one bonbon, a performance of the Bolshoi Ballet.

On the last day of their visit, an embassy colleague, Harry Barnes, and his wife, Betsy, joined Mimi and me in organizing a party for the American composers to which we invited Soviet composers and musicians whom the delegation had met or wanted to meet. We sent our invitations through the proper protocol channels, which meant they were vetted by the Ministry of Culture. To assure the Soviets that we meant nothing subversive, we also invited the ministry officials who had acted as "hosts" for the composers.

On the afternoon of the farewell party, one of the Soviet officials called me and stated flatly, "*Nam nie udobno*" ("It is inconvenient for us") to attend. When asked for whom it would be inconvenient, he replied, "For the Soviet guests." And indeed, none of them showed up. Consequently our American composers left the Soviet Union in some disgust, and Mimi and I had our first lesson in dealing with the Soviet bureaucracy.

When, two years later, the second U.S. delegation of composers came to Moscow—Aaron Copland and Lucas Foss—we asked Ambassador and Mrs. Llewellyn Thompson to host the farewell dinner at their residence. We had learned by that time that it was more difficult for the Soviets to snub the American ambassador as cavalierly as they had treated mere embassy staffers. As predicted, at the appointed hour Messrs. Khachaturian, Kabalevsky, and Shostakovich showed up—in the company, alas, of the uninvited Tikhon Khrennikov, whose only claim to musical fame was his position as chairman of the Union of Soviet Composers.

In fairness I should add that some of the negative impressions that the exchanges generated were not directly the fault of Soviet bureaucrats. In 1960, the painter Jimmy Ernst and the printmaker Rudy Pozzatti, who constituted the first delegation of American artists under the cultural agreement, became increasingly depressed during their four-week stay in the Soviet Union. To our surprise, they wanted to leave early, explaining that, as artists, they experience things primarily in a visual way. What depressed them so much was the absence, in that huge country, of anything visually interesting, original, or exciting that had been created since the Revolution. The stagnation in artistic creativity had utterly demoralized them.

Performing arts exchanges generally fared better. For one thing, they were the Soviets' trump card in their efforts to project themselves and their system to the American public. Indeed, the Bolshoi Ballet, the Kirov Ballet, the Moiseyev Folk Dance Ensemble, and several other first-rate performing arts groups created highly favorable impressions of Soviet culture in the United States. Most observers doubted, however, that such admiration translated—as the Soviets had presumably expected—into increasing acceptance in America of the Soviet political and social system.

The impact of American performing artists on the Soviet Union— in public diplomacy terms—is impossible to measure, even after fifty years. Yet, our objective of reaching a maximum number of Soviet people and having some interaction with them was certainly achieved through the appearance of outstanding American artists before crowds of interested Soviet concertgoers.

Hurok

Before discussing the appearance of individual American artists in the Soviet Union, I must explain the role that the legendary American impresario Sol Hurok played in the initial performing arts exchanges. In many respects Hurok was the man who made it happen. He often ignored the advice, and even the rules, that the State Department imposed on those promoting exchanges under the agreement. He frequently negotiated on his own with the Soviet cultural bureaucracy, yet he represented U.S. interests well. The Soviets respected him for his experience, artistic instinct, commercial acumen, and command of the ins and outs of the performing arts in the United States. He was of Ukrainian birth, spoke Russian, literally loved the great artists whom he represented, and was loved by them in return.

Hurok had what could only be called inordinate *chutzpah* in the way he went about his political and financial dealings with both American and Soviet officialdom. His was the grand manner, complete with bouquets of flowers, French perfume, Russian caviar, and the stiletto. By cajoling, threatening, persuading, and compromising with the authorities in both countries, he usually succeeded in making these artistic exchanges possible. He was responsible for bringing to the United States the Bolshoi and Kirov ballets, the Moiseyev, Ukrainian, and Georgian dance ensembles, and such musicians as David Oistrakh, Emil Gillels, and Sviatislav Richter. In return he sent "his" American artists—Isaac Stern, Byron Janis, Ruggiero Ricci, Roberta Peters, Mattiwilda Dobbs, and George London—to dazzle Soviet audiences. Despite the headaches he often caused officers in the State Department and the Moscow embassy, he was the one American impresario who could manage these exchanges so that they worked in both directions, satisfying both governments and the artists involved.

My first encounter with Hurok was typical of the way he worked. I received a call from him, informing me that Van Cliburn was arriving the next day. Cliburn, he told me, always traveled with his mother, but this time he would be alone—would I meet him at the airport and be his surrogate mother during his week's stay. So out to the airport I went.

There I found about 150 to 200 admirers with bouquets of flowers waiting to greet him. Ever since winning the Tchaikovsky piano competition six months earlier Cliburn had become Russia's darling. One can only compare the Van Cliburn mania with the Beatles madness. As soon as the plane had landed, the crowd of well-wishers—mostly women of all ages—broke through the barrier and rushed to the plane. A bewildered Cliburn emerged but quickly rose to the occasion and seemed to enjoy it immensely. It took a while for me to push through the throng to introduce myself and to whisk him off to the Hotel National, where another crowd of "groupies" had assembled to greet him.

And so it went for a week. Like royalty, Cliburn had to show himself frequently on his balcony to wave to his admirers. He was delightful to work with, although he latched onto me and practically wouldn't let me out of sight. His was a superb talent, and he played certain things—Tchaikovsky, Rachmaninoff—with great élan. That is what the Russians loved him for. But to my mind, at that time he still lacked insight into the composers of the classical period—Haydn, Mozart, Beethoven, Schubert. He played one sold-out concert with the Moscow State Philharmonic under Genadi Rozhdestvenski (Prokofiev no. 3 and Brahms no. 2) and gave one equally sold-out recital (Liszt, Barber, Rachmaninoff, Beethoven, and Chopin).

When I say "sold out," I don't mean that tickets were actually sold at the box office. One had to have real pull to get tickets for such elite performances, through political, social, or cultural organizations. Without such connections it was virtually impossible for the average Soviet citizen to attend a performance by an American artist. And, I should add, never, to the best of my knowledge, was there any advance press announcement or advertisement that an American artist was going to perform.

Hurok finally appeared on the scene and relieved me of my maternal duties. He came frequently to Moscow, usually to look after and entertain his artists and to arrange other performing arts exchanges with Goskonzert, the Soviet agency with which we dealt on all arts exchanges.

Isaac Stern came twice during my tour in Moscow. A wonderful artist and fun to be with, he and his long-time accompanist Alexander Zakin were greatly admired by Soviet audiences. In May 1960 he played three recitals and two concerts with the Moscow State Philharmonic (conducted by Evgenii Svetlanov), in which he performed the Mozart E-flat major, Bruch, Beethoven, Mendelsohn, and Brahms concertos in a near-marathon. During one recital, he announced a change in the program: "by popular request" he would play some unaccompanied Bach. Afterwards he told me that he just felt like playing a bit of Bach and that Alexander Zakin deserved a rest.

Sol Hurok (clowning) hosted a diner after a recital by Isaac Stern (far left) in the Hotel Metropol in Moscow, 1960. Soviet representative on Hurok's right, author on his left (American Embassy).

Isaac Stern and David Oistrakh during Stern's first tour of the Soviet Union under the U.S.-U.S.S.R. Cultural Exchange Agreement, May 1960 (American Embassy).

One of the pleasures of being with Isaac Stern was the opportunity to become acquainted with several great Soviet musicians, David Oistrakh, Emil Gilels, Sviatislav Richter, Mstislav Rostopovich, Vladimir Ashkenazi, and Leonid Kogan among them. Without Stern and Hurok, I, as an American diplomat, would never have had contact with them.

On one occasion, Leonid Kogan, who incidentally was suspected by some of his colleagues of being in cahoots with the security establishment, played a concerto by that hack of a composer, Tikhon Khrennikov, the aforementioned chairman of the Union of Soviet Composers. After the concert I asked Kogan whether he planned to play that concerto on an upcoming tour of America. He eyed me and then whispered, "Do you think I would play that piece anywhere but in the Soviet Union?" (An obituary in the *New York Times*, August 15, 2007, describes Khrennikov as "best known in the West as an official Soviet antagonist of Shostakovich and Prokofiev.")

On his 1960 tour, Isaac Stern had brought his wife Vera and their three-year old daughter Shira to Moscow. Shira had a birthday while there, and Isaac invited Mimi and me and some others to their suite in the Metropole Hotel for a proper birthday party. At the appropriate moment, he got out his fiddle, Emil Gilels sat down at the piano, and they played, as we all sang, "Happy Birthday to you . . ." It must have been in the musical economics of the day theoretically the most expensive rendering of that song ever performed.

Hurok's artists kept me pleasantly busy. Van Cliburn was followed by Byron Janis (playing Rachmaninoff and Gershwin with the Moscow State Symphony Orchestra) and Ruggiero Ricci (playing Bach, Beethoven, and Paganini, also with the Moscow State Symphony Orchestra). Mattiwilda Dobbs brought the house down singing Gilda in *Rigoletto* at the Bolshoi Opera, and Roberta Peters gave sparkling recitals in Moscow and Leningrad.

In Leningrad, where the audience wouldn't let Roberta go, despite encore after encore, I finally had to tell her that we had to leave to catch the night train back to Moscow. As we drove off, a crowd of fans ran after our limousine to the station and stood in front of the window of our compartment, cheering and waving until the train departed. Roberta turned to me and said, "I wish they treated me like that in New York."

An engaging young American pianist, Daniel Pollack, who had competed unsuccessfully in the Tchaikovsky Competition, gave several fine recitals. Some years later when Mimi and I were in Bulgaria, we invited him to come to Sofia to repeat his success.

George London was the last of the American artists to come to Moscow during our tour there. He sang the title role in *Boris Godunov*, the first foreign artist to perform that role at the Bolshoi Opera. In the last scene, as Czar Boris dies, London literally tumbled from his throne onto the stage floor in a scary but well rehearsed, authentic-looking fall, creating at first a loud gasp on the part of the audience, which then, as one collective, jumped to its feet and became, in a near-riot, a mass of cheering, feet-stomping people.

The New York Philharmonic in Russia

The first major American performing arts presentation under the U.S.-Soviet Cultural Agreement of 1958 was the New York Philharmonic, which came to the Soviet Union in August 1959. Directed by Leonard Bernstein, alternating with guest conductor Thomas Shippers, the Philharmonic played eight concerts in Moscow, Leningrad, and Kiev. The programs were a mixture of standard classical and contemporary American compositions. Seymour Lipkin was the piano soloist in some of the concerts.

Thomas Shippers conducting the New York Philharmonic in the Moscow Conservatory Hall, August 1959 (Columbia Records).

Cheers and rhythmic clapping acclaimed the orchestra wherever they played, and Bernstein quickly rose to the position of "Mr. American Music." Lenny, as he became known to everyone who met him, performed on and off the stage with enthusiasm and personal generosity. Mimi and I accompanied the orchestra on their tour of the three cities and were immediately embraced into Lenny's and his wife Felicia's family of friends and fellow travelers. There was never a dull moment while we were traveling, at dinners after the concerts, or during intermission in his dressing room, where instead of resting he welcomed anyone who came to greet him.

Somehow, Thomas Shippers, the brilliant, young upcoming conductor, was not included in Lenny's embrace of intimates. There was certainly no enmity but perhaps a bit of envy on Lenny's part in seeing the 28-year-old Shippers's success as a mirror of his own budding career thirteen years earlier. That was pure conjecture on my part and in no way did I see any effect on their artistic association.

The orchestra's tour in the Soviet Union coincided with the mammoth American National Exhibition in Moscow, another principal element of the U.S.-Soviet Cultural Agreement. The exhibition, spread over several pavilions in Moscow's Sokolniki Park, drew tens of thousands of visitors every day. When Bernstein

Leonard Bernstein's birthday party in the Hotel Ukraina in Moscow, August 1959. On his right, his wife, Felicia; on his left, the author's wife, Mimi (Carl Mydans for Life Magazine*).*

visited the show, he was immediately surrounded by a throng of well-wishers, clamoring for his autograph. He did better than that: he distributed LPs of the Philharmonic that he had brought along for the occasion. The commotion thereby created called forth the Soviet police, who were only too eager to interfere in the smooth operation of the exhibition by claiming crowd-control responsibilities.

Mimi and I organized a birthday party for Lenny—his forty-first, although he claimed it was his fortieth—in the dining room of the Ukraina Hotel, where the orchestra was staying. We invited a number of our American friends, including *Life* correspondent Carl Mydans and his wife Shelly. As Carl never went anywhere without his camera, the result some weeks later was a feature in *Life* magazine, "*Life* Goes to a Birthday Party in Moscow."

The last day of the Philharmonic's visit turned out to be a triumph for Lenny and the orchestra with far greater impact than anyone had anticipated. What happened is recorded in a *New York Times* op-ed piece of March 14, 1987, authored by me and reprinted here:

"A 'Nonperson" Named Boris Pasternak

Bethesda, Md. —The Soviet Government's rehabilitation of Boris Pasternak recalls an event involving the great Russian writer that turned out to be a dramatic and deeply moving moment for those who witnessed it in Moscow in September 1959.

It occurred at a time when Mr. Pasternak was in total official disgrace. He had become a nonperson in the eyes of the Soviet leadership, even as Nikita S. Khrushchev was creating the first thaw in the winter of Communist orthodoxy.

Mr. Pasternak had not been permitted to accept the Nobel Prize; he was isolated in his country home in Peredelkino, a writers' colony near Moscow, and he had not been seen in public in about six months. The only evidence that he was still on people's minds and continued to be admired was the whispered requests for *Doctor Zhivago*, his banned novel, copies of which were in the hands of some Westerners who shared them with their eager Russian friends.

The New York Philharmonic, under the direction of Leonard Bernstein, had been performing that year in Moscow, Leningrad and Kiev— the first major visit by a musical organization after the signing of the United States-Soviet Cultural Exchange Agreement in 1958. The orchestra had been enthusiastically, even emotionally, received everywhere it appeared, and it returned to Moscow to perform a final gala concert.

Mr. Bernstein had said the one thing he wanted to do before leaving the Soviet Union was to visit Mr. Pasternak's dacha in Peredelkino, which he did the day before the concert. It was reportedly a gracious and warm meeting, and at the end Mr. Bernstein invited Mr. Pasternak and his wife to his concert the next evening, not expecting, however, that they would be able to attend such a public event.

The day of the concert was hectic. It began with a filming of one of Mr. Bernstein's Omnibus television programs at Moscow's Conservatory Hall, with the New York Philharmonic on stage and an invited audience of enthusiastic music students and musicians.

By 7:45 p.m., the sold-out Conservatory was jammed— this time with an elite audience that had managed somehow to get tickets for this final concert. Suddenly, as if on a single cue, every eye in the hall appeared to focus on two people sitting in the center of the auditorium. Boris Pasternak was easily recognizable with his white hair and sharply lined facial features. Everyone in the concert hall, from orchestra to second balcony, zeroed in on Mr. Pasternak and his wife.

It was as if there was no one else there—and certainly no one that mattered—only the two Pasternaks sitting quietly as if it were the most natural thing for the two political exiles to attend a concert in Moscow. There was a subdued buzzing in the hall as people motioned to one another and stared.

The tension, almost unbearable in its intensity, was broken suddenly when Mr. Bernstein appeared on stage, followed by a tremendous cheer. Some of those present, perhaps including Mr. Bernstein, were sure that at least part of the enthusiastic greeting was meant to be shared by Mr. Pasternak.

During intermission, Mr. Pasternak went backstage, and he and Mr. Bernstein talked for about 10 minutes, Mr. Pasternak coming out of his shell of reserve and, speaking animatedly, apologizing for his 'rusty' English, which turned out to be fluent if stylistically antiquated. Mr. Bernstein was excited and effusive as ever, full of embraces and grateful for the writer's compliments. A photo of Mr. Pasternak today serves as record of the event.

The second half of the program was to be the climax of the entire tour. At the conclusion of Shostakovich's Fifth Symphony, the composer came onto the stage to share the rhythmic applause of the audience that continued for some 30 minutes. During the ovation, Mr. Pasternak and his wife slipped quietly and practically unnoticed out of the hall, never, to my knowledge, to be publicly seen again.

To at least one member of the audience that evening, what stands out today as the Soviet leaders rehabilitate the great writer, is the memory of Mr. Pasternak being momentarily recognized in Conservatory Hall as simply a warm, welcome and appreciative guest.

I rarely carry a camera, but I had brought one with me intending to take a few pictures of Lenny from backstage as he conducted the orchestra. When I asked Mr. Pasternak to come backstage during the intermission to greet Lenny, he at first demurred, suggesting that he did not wish to disturb him. I told him that Lenny would appreciate a short visit from him, and while they chatted, I snapped photos, one of which (included in this book) I thought quite representative of Pasternak.

Boris Pasternak during intermission of the last concert of the New York Philharmonic in Moscow, August 1959 (H. N. Tuch).

Other Visitors of Note

Two other American performing arts groups visited the Soviet Union during my tour of duty in Moscow. One was the touring company of *My Fair Lady*, which was then running on Broadway. Featuring Lola Fisher as Eliza (whom critics praised as an equal to Julie Andrews) and, alternately, Edward Mulcahy and Michael Evans as Henry Higgins, the show was a terrific success and an eye opener to Russians, who were largely unfamiliar with American musicals. Franz Allers, the conductor of the original Broadway production, led all sixteen performances in Moscow, Leningrad, and Kiev.

The other performing arts group, a different sort, was the University of Michigan Concert Band. Under its renowned bandmaster, William Ravelli, the band was rather unexpectedly a great success. Their musical artistry, their discipline, and their youthful enthusiasm were impressive, and the willingness of the students to meet and mix it up with young Russians, while disturbing to the security apparatus, left a lasting good impression wherever they appeared. They went farther afield than the usual tri-city tour of Moscow-Leningrad-Kiev, traveling to several provincial cities not previously visited by American arts groups.

Finally, shortly after the Tuch family left the Soviet Union in 1961, the Robert Shaw Chorale visited Moscow and Leningrad under the U.S,-Soviet Cultural Agreement. I was back in Moscow for the occasion and heard them perform the Bach B Minor Mass, which was truly thrilling.

The British, I should add, not to be outdone by the Americans, brought the Royal Ballet to Moscow in 1961 while we were there. Featuring Margot Fonteyn and Michael Somes, the company performed *Sleeping Beauty*, as well as *La Fille Mal Garde* with Nadia Nerina, David Blair, and Alexander Grant, and *Undine*, a ballet by Hans Werner Henze, featuring the young Svetlana Beriosova. From England also came the Old Vic with a production of Shakespeare's *Macbeth*, with Paul Rogers and Barbara Jefford.

Russian Artists

During our three years in Moscow, we heard some of Moscow's and Leningrad's finest in music. I shall mention here only the highlights.

Opera Russian opera productions at the Bolshoi were impressive both vocally (by the male lower voices) and visually. We heard *Boris Godunov* and *Prince Igor* with I. I. Petrov, the reigning basso. I did have problems with most of the women's voices, whether as soloists or in chorus. They favored a type of nasal singing, an apparent Russian tradition prevailing at a time when artists had not yet been exposed to Western training.

Orchestras We were able to hear about a dozen concerts by the Moscow State Philharmonic under Kiril Kondrashin, Evgenii Svetlanov, Kurt Zanderling, and Konstantin Ivanov, with David Oistrakh, Emil Gilels, Leonid Kogan, and Vladimir Ashkenazi as soloists. In Leningrad, we heard the Leningrad Philharmonic under E. A. Mavrinsky, then considered the premiere orchestra in the Soviet Union and one of the finest anywhere. Their hall, the Leningrad Philharmonic, is even today considered acoustically one of the best in existence.

One of the most memorable of the many wonderful concerts we heard was one of contemporary music during the visit of Aaron Copland and Lucas Foss. The Moscow State Symphony played

Copland's Symphony no. 2, conducted by the composer; Lucas Foss's Piano Concerto no. 2, conducted by Copland and played by the composer; and Shostakovich's Symphony no. 9, conducted by Alexander Gauk. There was real and spontaneous conviviality among the artists and listeners during and after the concert.

Ballet I did an actual count and came up with two dozen performances we attended by the Bolshoi Ballet. Among the standards were half a dozen *Swan Lakes*, two with Maya Plisetskaya; several *Chopinianas* with Bessmertnova, Sorokina, Kondratyeva, and Timofeyeva; and *Cinderella* with Struchkova. Several novelties included the Soviet propaganda ballet, *The Red Flower*; *Stone Flower* (music by Prokofiev) with Maksimova; the *Humpback Horse* with Plisetskaya and music by her husband, V. Shchedrin; and *Paganini* (music by Rachmaninoff).

By sheer luck, we were present when Galina Ulanova gave her last performance before retirement in 1959. She was in her fifties but still looked and acted like a young girl, dancing the third act of *Romeo and Juliet*.

The leading ballerinas of the Bolshoi Ballet arriving in New York in April 1959. From left: Ekaterina Maximova, Marina Kondratieva, Maya Plisetskaya, Raissa Struchkova, Liudmila Bogomolova, Nina Timofeyeva (courtesy of Sol Hurok).

Plisetskaya, incidentally, was initially not permitted to come with the Bolshoi Ballet on its first visit to the United States. She was evidently considered too independent and politically unreliable to be permitted to leave the Soviet Union. Hurok, however, raised such a fuss, threatening to cancel the whole tour, that the authorities relented and permitted the prima ballerina to join the company. And audiences, of course, loved her everywhere she danced.

In Moscow, we also attended the Bolshoi's main competition, the Stanislavsky Theater Ballet, which prided itself on having the currently best male dancer, Maris Liepa. For unexplained but probably political reasons, Liepa was not permitted to dance at the Bolshoi. The Moiseyev State Folk Dance Ensemble, which was such a hit in the United States as one of Hurok's presentations under the Agreement, performed in Moscow as probably the most outstanding original folk dance company in the country.

I had a long conversation with Moiseyev after his troupe returned from the United States. He was full of praise for what he saw and experienced in America and critical of Soviet restrictions. I reported the conversation in a confidential dispatch to the State Department. Someone in Washington leaked it to the *New York Times* which, to my dismay, reprinted it in large part. My friend, Max Frankel, the *New York Times* Moscow correspondent, was as chagrined as I was and apologized to me. Mr. Moiseyev never spoke to me again.

During my frequent visits to Leningrad, I always tried to attend a performance of the Kirov Ballet, the other principal ballet company in the Soviet Union and considered by many the superior in upholding the nineteenth-century Russian ballet tradition. It wasn't easy: the company was often not performing or on tour or in rotation with the Kirov Opera, since both performed in the beautiful Maryinsky Theater. I did succeed in seeing a very traditional and beautiful *Swan Lake* and two of the Kirov's so-called "modern" productions—*Spartak* and *The Bronze Horseman*—which I found tedious in their emphasis on athleticism and posturing.

I attended ballet performances in Kiev, Tbilisi, Odessa, Yerevan, and in the distant "closed" city of Novosibirsk, the latter only by virtue of being a member of Vice President Nixon's entourage during his visit to the Soviet Union in August 1959.

Soviet Musicians. I mentioned earlier the recitals by American artists in Moscow—Van Cliburn, Isaac Stern, Ruggiero Ricci, Roberta Peters, Mattiwilda Dobbs, and Byron Janis—but so far have written little about the Soviet artists whose recitals echo in my ear to this day. Emil Gilels (playing Mozart, Beethoven, and Schubert) and the young Vladimir Ashkenazi (playing Mozart and Schumann) were among the admirable artists we heard in recital.

I attended several appearances by Sviatislav Richter, playing Haydn, Beethoven, Brahms, Liszt, Schimanovsky, and Prokofiev. Richter was an unpredictable performer, often changing programs midstream and playing what he felt like, but always with ethereal feeling and emotional intensity. At one performance he came onstage, did not acknowledge the applause of the audience, crossed himself, sat down, and started playing as though he were the only person in the hall. On the day Boris Pasternak died and throngs of mourners passed through his house in Peredelkino to pay their respects, Richter sat there at an upright piano playing Bach continuously for a reported nine hours straight.

Tours of duty for embassy officers in Moscow had been strictly limited to two years for a long time. Ambassador Thompson believed, however, that it took that long to become thoroughly familiar with the Soviet scene and that the experience of a third year of duty would make the officer more valuable in terms of observation, contacts, and reporting. When he asked if I would stay for a third year, I was so flattered to be asked anything by "Tommy" Thompson, my first of three role models, that I immediately agreed and then went home to break the news to Mimi. Along with other embassy wives, she carried the real burdens of this hardship post. To my surprise and relief, Mimi, who was somewhat of a conservative in lifestyle if not in politics, quickly agreed, saying, "Anything is better than another change of posts."

Russian Theater. We spent much of our third year in Moscow becoming acquainted with the Russian theater, inspired by Norris Houghton, who had come on a three-month visit under the Cultural Exchange Agreement. Houghton was director of the Phoenix Theater in New York and America's foremost expert on the Russian theater. He had authored the seminal work *Moscow Rehearsal* in 1936, based on his Moscow theater experience in 1934–35. He came back to Moscow to observe the current state of the Russian stage and to assess the evolution of theater productions in Moscow since the days of Stanislavsky, Meierhold, and Vakhtangov. His knowledge was indeed profound, and he was an engaging teacher and companion for Mimi and me as we tried to learn to appreciate Russian classics at the Moscow Art Theater and the Maly Theater: Chekhov's *Three Sisters, Cherry Orchard, Ivanov, The Seagull*; the plays of the Satire Theater: Mayakovsky's *Klop* (*The Bedbug*), and Ilf-Petrov's *Twelve Chairs*; and the productions of the Gorky Theater, the Gogol Theater, the Vachtangov Theater, and the

Sovremenek (Contemporary) Theater, which was frequently closed by the security authorities for violating Communist orthodoxy. He gave us a list of about twenty plays that we were "instructed" to see, and we did our best to follow orders during the nine remaining months of our tour.

Houghton subsequently published *Return Engagement,* which he subtitled *A Postscript to 'Moscow Rehearsals.*[7] We found particularly interesting his observation on the enervating lengths of current presentations of the classics, such as the Moscow Art Theater (MXAT) production of Chekhov's *Three Sisters.* In an attempt to remain true to the Stanislavsky tradition, Houghton said, the MXAT actors and their directors, over time and with repetition, dragged out the play to a length of four hours, when the original had been no longer than two and a half hours. Not ever having experienced the play as originally conceived, we finally understood why it seemed so interminably boring when we first saw it at the MXAT. ("Boring" — or "skuchno" in Russian — incidentally seemed to be Chekhov's favorite word in *Three Sisters,* occurring as it does several times in practically every scene.)

During 1960 and 1961, we were able to get away from Moscow once each year — both times to Frankfurt. On our first "recreation and rehabilitation" trip we were able to hear Georg Solti conduct a memorable performance of Richard Strauss's *Electra* with a triple hit team of Christl Goltz, Margarete Klose (who must have been in her mid-sixties by that time), and Gladys Kuchta. On our second trip out to Frankfurt in 1961, we heard Mozart's *Die Entfuehrung aus dem Serail.* The only reason I remember that performance and mention it here is because it was the first time we heard Anja Silja, who was then twenty-one years old but already a "star."

Politics

Our three years in Moscow, as noted earlier, reflected the roller coaster in political relations between the United States and the Soviet Union. Our arrival in1958 coincided with the beginning of "the Spirit of Camp David," an initial, gradual thawing in U.S.-Soviet relations, generated by Chairman Khrushchev's visit to the United States that year. The Khrushchev-Eisenhower meeting was to be reciprocated by an Eisenhower visit to the Soviet Union in the spring of 1960. Preparations for the visit had been fully completed (including the construction of a four-hole golf course in Irkutsk for the president, who was expected to stop there before exiting the Soviet Union on his way to Japan). An entire test trip from Moscow to Leningrad to Kiev to Irkutsk, in which I participated, had already been completed, when, on May 1, the Soviets shot down Gary Power's U-2 and plunged U.S-Soviet relations into the lower depths.

The election of President Kennedy in November 1960 and friendly exchanges between Krushchev and the new president seemed to lift bilateral relations again, only to have them drop back down as the result of the Bay of Pigs invasion in April 1961. The relationship was not improved by the destructive meeting between the two leaders in Vienna in July 1961, when they seemed to disagree on everything, and Khrushchev treated Kennedy boorishly (causing the president to turn to Ambassador Thompson, who had asked to leave Moscow after his four years there, and remark, "Now I understand why you want to get out of that hellhole").

I can't end this account of our Moscow post without for a moment exchanging my cultural attaché "hat" for that of my press attaché role, and relating what was probably the major political event during my tour: the visit of Vice President Richard Nixon in August 1959 to open the U.S. National Exhibition in Moscow and to visit the Soviet Union in advance of the then-planned trip of President Eisenhower. I participated as press aide to Herbert Klein, the vice president's press secretary, in "handling" the 125-odd American correspondents accompanying the vice president. The incident that has carved Mr. Nixon's visit in history was the famous "Kitchen Debate" between the vice president and Nikita Khrushchev on the day the exhibition was inaugurated.

For years, William Safire, the retired *New York Times* columnist and former Nixon administration official, has contended in his published writings that it was he who had engineered the debate as a public relations coup on behalf of the company that had constructed the model house with the famous kitchen. The facts as I recall them, from being present at the occasion, are different.

Richard Nixon, in conducting Nikita Khrushchev through a preview of the exhibition before its formal opening, led him first to the RCA color television studio, where a video taping of the two in conversation was demonstrated. (This was for the Soviets such a new technological development that the video head was locked up nightly in my embassy safe to protect it from anticipated theft.) While the two talked for the video cameras, Mr. Khrushchev became increasingly aggressive, but Mr. Nixon remained restrained. As we emerged from the studio, Mr. Nixon turned to those of us escorting the party, saying that as the host he felt he should be polite, but then added: "What gives with him? If he starts that again, I'll let him have it."

Vice President Richard Nixon with Soviet Chairman Nikita Khrushchev at the American National Exhibition in Moscow, minutes before the famed "kitchen debate." In rear stands the Buckminster Fuller Geodesic Dome, the center of the exhibition. From left: the author; John Scali, then AP correspondent; George Allen, USIA director; Alex Akalovsky, Nixon's interpreter; Chairman Khrushchev; Chad McClanahan, director general of the exhibition; Vice President Nixon (United States Embassy).

The next stop on the tour was a walk-through of a model of a "typical" American one-family home along a path that cut the house into two halves. As we stopped to look at the kitchen, Khrushchev again launched into polemics, and this time Nixon gave tit for tat. They were surrounded by a crowd of American photographers and reporters snapping pictures and scribbling furiously. To the best of my knowledge there is no verbatim record of the "debate,"only what the newsmen pieced together either directly or from the interpreters. (Tape recorders were not yet a common gadget.)

The "bout" lasted 15 to 20 minutes. Every time it looked as though they were going into a real "clinch," they backed off, laughed, embraced, and then went at it again—a fascinating confrontation that was, however, a pure historical accident, not a

Chairman Khrushchev admonishing the author about American contemporary art at the American National Exhibition in Moscow, August 1959 (United States Embassy).

cleverly planned Safire public relations coup for the construction company he represented. In "recognition" of my presence at the event, the vice president presented me with a certificate identifying me a member of his "Kitchen Cabinet."

Chairman Khruschev returned to the exhibition a week later for another visit, this time accompanied by Anastas Mikoyan. He wanted to see the art exhibit. As the only American official present, I was drawn in as guide and interpreter. He looked approvingly at the examples of nineteenth century American artwork—Church, Bierstadt, Homer, Bellows—(which, incidentally had been personally selected for the exhibition by President Eisenhower in response to congressional criticism that the show would include exclusively contemporary "abstract" art.) When Khrushchev came upon a work by John Marin and I explained its title, "Sea and Sky," he remarked, "It looks as though someone peed on the canvas." Stuttering, I translated, "The chairman said it appeared to him that a little boy had made a puddle on the canvas." Khrushchev inquired,

During Vice President Nixon's visit to the Soviet Union in 1959, he and his party traveled to the then "closed" city of Sverdlovsk (Now, again, Ekaterininburg). While walking in the city, I came across the building— photographed here—on the roof of which the last photograph of Tsar Nicholas and his family was taken shortly before their execution. The building was subsequently razed (H. N. Tuch).

and was told, how his comment had been interpreted, whereupon he admonished, "Please interpret the chairman correctly." I said, "It looks as though someone had peed on the canvas."

Khrushchev's comments grew increasingly critical as he viewed the works of contemporary American artists, culminating in an angry outburst—perhaps calculated, perhaps real—upon seeing the large female nude statue by Gaston Lachaise (from New York's Museum of Modern Art) that was the centerpiece of the sculpture garden. He shouted, in Russian, "Only a pederast could have done this." And he rushed off, followed by his entourage.

The American National Exhibition was a huge exposition, planned and coordinated by the U.S. Information Agency and assisted by a number of major American corporations, including Pepsi-Cola and Coty. Designed to present to the Soviet public for the first time a comprehensive view of America, the exhibition featured the latest in U.S. home and entertainment technology (including the RCA color television studio), science, fashions, American family living (the model house with *the* kitchen), consumer products, photography (Edward Steichen's "Family of Man"), and a gallery of late nineteenth and twentieth century American art. The centerpiece was a Buckminster Fuller geodesic dome that contained a gigantic seven-screen film projection depicting a 24-hour period in the lives of typical Americans living in various parts of the United States. To this day, the exhibition is remembered by some of the more than one million Soviet visitors as their first glimpse of America. In America it is remembered as the site of the Khrushchev-Nixon confrontation.

The American Correspondents in Moscow

As far as the Soviet authorities were concerned, the small American media correspondents corps was part of the "U.S. spy network" in Moscow and was often treated as such. We included them—and they included us—in our beleaguered American community and tried to support each other professionally and socially. In my capacity as press attaché, I served as their embassy contact, a task that was informal and congenial and resulted in close and lasting personal friendships with several of the journalists and their families.

Though we probably didn't realize it at the time, our American correspondents group was an exceptionally distinguished one. Among the radio correspondents, John Chancellor represented NBC, and Marvin Kalb CBS; the *New York Times* had Osgood Carruthers and Max Frankel; Tom Lambert was the *New York Herald Tribune's* correspondent, and Pete Kumpa the *Baltimore Sun's*. Carl Mydans (later Howard Sochurek) represented *Life* magazine. Harold (Heini) Milk headed the AP bureau. Robert "Bud" Korngold, later a USIA colleague, and Aileen Mosby, who had a horrible, if typical, experience at the hands of KGB goons, served in the UP bureau. The two longest-serving American journalists in Moscow were Henry Shapiro, heading the UP bureau, and Ed Stevens, representing *Time* magazine and the *Christian Science Monitor*. Both had been in Moscow since the 1930s, causing some of their colleagues to regard them with some ambivalence: was their longevity related to compromises they had to make with the regime? (Ed Stevens's wife Nina, a Russian native, owned a large, beautiful log cabin in the middle of Moscow—the only such private residence that I was aware of. She and Ed entertained there lavishly; their guests included Soviet officials, journalists, artists, writers, and foreign visitors. At one of the dinner parties that Mimi and I attended, the guest of honor was none other that Eleanor Roosevelt.)

During our first year in Moscow, the correspondents were forced to submit their stories to the censors before they could be transmitted to their home offices. The censors were located at the *Tsentralni Telegraf* on Gorky Street, and each evening the correspondents gathered there, submitting their dispatches through a slot in a blacked-out window, never getting a look at whoever played God with their dispatches. They waited there for their stories to be cleared, a period that could take several hours. I frequently joined the group as they sat around and waited, exchanging news and gossip. (In 1959, during one of the periodic thaws in U.S.-Soviet relations, the procedure was changed, and the correspondents were permitted to file dispatches directly from their offices.)

None of the American journalists had ever caught sight of their censorious tormentors. Tom Lambert, before leaving Moscow on reassignment, decided to do something about that. Lambert purchased two tickets, in addition to his own, to the Bolshoi Theater and passed them through the slot, thus extending an invitation to his censor as a token of his appreciation for the latter's prompt service to the *Herald Tribune*. On the appointed evening, Tom and Helen Lambert went to the Bolshoi only to find that the designated seats remained empty throughout the performance.

On Friday afternoons the American correspondents were invited to come to the Embassy for an informal off-the-record chat with Ambassador Thompson. On one such day, Priscilla Johnson (later MacMillan), a stringer for the North American Newspaper Alliance (NANA), stopped by my office on the way up to the chat and asked whether there was anything new or interesting. I told her that earlier that afternoon, Richard Snyder, our consular officer, had come up to my office complaining about this "crazy American" who had come to the Embassy insisting that he wanted to give up his citizenship. Snyder said he tried to talk the man out of his decision and finally told him to think about it over the weekend and come back on Monday if he really wanted to go through with it. Since the man was staying at the Metropole Hotel, where Priscilla was housed, I suggested she might want to talk to him for a possible story, and so she did.

The man was Lee Harvey Oswald. Since Priscilla had earlier worked in John Kennedy's presidential campaign, where she met the candidate, she may be the one person—as far as I know—who formed a human link between the president and his assassin. (Priscilla became a close friend and supporter to Harvey's widow, Marina Oswald.)

The U-2 Crisis

I simply can't leave my Moscow service without recalling what several of my colleagues consider my singular diplomatic success story. On May 1, 1960, when the Soviets announced that an American spy plane had been shot down, they did not indicate where the U-2 aircraft had been downed. Washington was scrambling frantically with supposedly innocent explanations; even President Eisenhower was dissembling by claiming that the plane had merely strayed across the Turkish border.

That evening the Soviet Union of Journalists had a First of May party, to which I, as press attaché , had been invited for the first time during our stay. When I arrived, I was immediately surrounded by a number of acquaintances who berated me about the alleged spy plane. I said something to the effect that, no matter what, it was an unfriendly act to shoot down the plane of a friendly nation. One young reporter whom I knew blurted out, "What should we have done, Gospodin Tuch? The plane was flying over Sverdlovsk" (more than a thousand miles from "the Turkish border"). Taken aback, I asked, "Where did you say?" whereupon everyone disappeared from the scene.

I departed quickly, went straight to Spaso House, roused Ambassador Thompson, and reported what I had heard. He told me to find the embassy communicator and get the information to Washington immediately, adding in his laconic way, "I think they'll want to hear that as soon as possible."

4

Washington 1961–1965

In August 1961 we returned to Washington, relieved to be finally released from the stifling atmosphere of constant harassment and suspicion that an assignment in the Soviet Union then represented, yet appreciative of the cultural, artistic, and professional experiences we enjoyed during our three years in Moscow.

My new job was exiting and fulfilling. As one of the assistants to Edward R.Murrow, the legendary radio news reporter and TV commentator, whom President Kennedy had appointed director of the U.S. Information Agency, I had the responsibility of initiating and supervising U.S. public diplomacy programs in the Soviet Union and Eastern Europe and advising Murrow on policies toward the area.

Ed Murrow became my second role model (joining Tommy Thompson). He insisted that his area assistants spend half their time in the countries for which they were responsible. I had no intention of spending six months of the year in the hellhole from which I had just emerged, but I did take the opportunity to visit Eastern Europe and to return to the Soviet Union on short trips whenever the occasion presented itself. Thus I jumped at the chance to be the State Department escort for George Balanchine's New York City Ballet on its first tour of Russia in the fall of 1962.

The schedule called for the company to perform in Moscow, Leningrad, Kiev, Tbilisi, and Baku. It is hard to describe the success and choreographic revelations the company enjoyed. Every one of their appearances was met with prolonged rhythmic applause and cheering, although, as per Soviet practice vis-a-vis American performance arts groups, never with critical comment in the press. I won't list all the ballets they performed—they included *Serenade*, *Agon*, *Western Symphony*, *Symphony in C*, *Scottish Symphony*, *Concerto Barocco*, *Prodigal Son*, and *La Valse*—and the artists were among the cream of the crop of American dancers: Jacque d'Amboise,

The New York City Ballet with choreographer George Balanchine (at far left); group photo taken in Baku before departure from the Soviet Union, December 1962 (New York City Ballet).

Melissa Hayden, Allegra Kent, Conrad Ludlow, Patricia McBride, Nicholas Magallanes, Francisco Moncion, Edward Villella, Patricia Wilde, Violette Verdi, Arthur Mitchell, Gloria Govrin, Patricia Neary, and three teenage future stars, then members of the corps de ballet, Susan Farrell, Kay Mazzo, and Marnee Morris, travelling under their mothers' watchful eyes.

One of the remembered pleasures of the trip was meeting and spending time with Lincoln Kirstein, the cofounder, codirector, principal financial sustainer, and artistic inspiration of the New York City Ballet (and the American School of Ballet), who was along on the trip. While most of the members of the company showed little interest in the cultural attractions that the cities we visited offered — the museums, the architectural monuments — Lincoln Kirstein was a delightful companion on these excursions.

George Balanchine was always friendly and polite, but personally somewhat remote. He had a phenomenal Svengali-like control over his ensemble. His dancers seemed totally committed to him, striving for perfection merely to please him. He would stand backstage watching, usually with a smiling nod or short word of encouragement and approval. Amazingly, when Balanchine had to return briefly to New York, the company practically fell apart. Everything went wrong during the performances: the dancers kept falling, the staging was off, cues were missed. The minute Balanchine came back, everything returned to near-perfection.

Balanchine was lionized by the Soviets as a native son— "nash Georgii" (our George)—at receptions and gatherings with Soviet artists. He would have none of that. Tired of this constant misintroduction, he responded on one occasion, in Russian, "I am not your Georgii. If I had remained your Georgii, we would dance as badly as you do!"

Then, in a previously unscheduled afternoon performance for students in Moscow, Balanchine included Webern's *Episodes*. It amazed and delighted the audience. Afterward, Balanchine was accosted backstage by Ministry of Culture functionaries who advised him not to repeat the ballet during the tour. He asked why, and they explained that "our experts" consider it inappropriate for Soviet audiences, that they would not understand and therefore could not appreciate it. He then asked who were the "experts" giving such advice. The answer was the Culture Ministry officials. Balanchine—again in Russian—calmly told them, "[expletive] your experts" and turned away.

Indeed, many in the Soviet audiences did not understand Balanchine's abstract ballets. Used to concrete, story-telling ballets, perplexed balletgoers kept asking the dancers what it all meant; they were sure that there had to be a story in, say, *Serenade*. To satisfy their curiosity, some of the dancers made up elaborate "scenarios," to wit, the first scene in *Serenade* represented a subway car where riders were holding on to the overhead straps. A late passenger enters and not finding an empty strap, searches until she locates one. In another scene, the take-off of a new model Thunderbird with its passengers is simulated. The "scenarios" became increasingly more imaginative when the dancers realized that their explanations met with apparent acceptance and increased the literal-minded Soviet public's appreciation for the ballets.

One evening before a performance, I encountered Arthur Mitchell, the only black dancer in the company, standing in front of a full-length mirror, dressed in a princely white costume. He was taking the place of Jacques d'Amboise, who had been slightly injured in an accident in Hamburg before the company came to the Soviet Union and was not yet dancing again. I told him he looked great and all would go well in his new role. "I just have to remember one thing," he said. "What's that?" I asked. "Think white!" he replied.

My principal contribution to the ballet's success was noteworthy. The dancers had constantly complained about the food they were served, not so much the quality or quantity but the variety. I traveled back to Moscow weekly to check in with the embassy and to pick up the company's accumulated mail. On my return, I always brought with me a case of peanut butter and placed a jar on every table of the dining room where the dancers ate their dinner after the performance. I was hailed as Mr. Peanut Butter, the ballet's savior!

The Soviet media did not advertise the ballet's tour, but somehow word of mouth spread the news so that there were always long lines of people clamoring for tickets. I don't think there was ever a vacant seat at any of the performances in the cities where the company appeared. The reaction, even to the most abstract ballets — *Agon* or *Concerto Barocco* — was uniformly enthusiastic and admiring of the choreography and the technical and expressive perfection of the dancers.

For me, the event that stands out in my memory of the five-week tour was that we were in Leningrad during the Cuban missile crisis in October 1962 and were completely oblivious of the dangerous situation. The Soviet authorities had restricted all American diplomats to Moscow when the crisis started. Since I was not a member of the embassy staff, they had apparently forgotten that I was with the ballet, and thus it turned out that I was the only American diplomat outside of Moscow during the crisis. Together with the dancers, George Balanchine and Lincoln Kirstein, I was enjoying the sights of Leningrad, happy in the glow of admiration and appreciation of everyone we encountered.

When I received an urgent phone call from the embassy, asking about the mood in the city and the attitude of the Soviets vis-à-vis the Americans in their midst, I replied everything was fine, we were enjoying *mir i druzhba* (peace and friendship) and great success in the ballet's appearances on and off the stage. My incredulous interlocutors asked whether I knew what was going on "on the outside." I expressed ignorance, admitting that the batteries in the shortwave radio I always carried with me were dead. "Why do you ask?" I countered. "Get some batteries and listen to the Voice of America," I was told. Only then did I learn about the immediacy of the crisis, which fortunately came to an end a day later.

There had been nothing about the crisis in the Soviet media. The Soviet population, like us, appeared to be in complete ignorance of the dangers of a nuclear confrontation that was the concern of practically everyone living outside the Soviet Bloc, especially in the United States. I only realized the extent of the fear that prevailed in the United States when some days later I received a letter from Mimi, advising me to head eastward, out of the reach of the nuclear bombs that might be headed for the major cities of the Soviet Union.

Ignorance is bliss, one might conclude. Yet this was a vivid example of the two worlds we lived in—one free to know what was going on, the other closed to all information except what the authorities wanted people to know.

Back in Washington Mimi and I began to enjoy the many musical offerings the capital provided, starting with the twenty-four concerts of the Juilliard Quartet at the Library of Congress that we attended during the four years we spent in the capital. The Juillard Quartet (consisting of the violinists Robert Mann and Isidore Cohen, the violist Rafael Hillyer and the cellist Claus Adam) had succeeded the Budapest String Quartet as the resident quartet of the Library, performing on the Library's collection of rare Stradivari instruments. Their schedule called for six concerts per year, playing in the Library's Coolidge Auditorium.

We were able to attend all of them, thanks to our friendship with Rafael Hillyer, who provided us with tickets. (Though only twenty-five cents, tickets to these concerts were normally difficult to obtain, requiring early Monday morning phone calls and waiting on the line to reserve seats.) We usually met Rafe after the concerts, either to get a bite to eat or to take him to Union Station for his late train back to New York.

Concerts were often attended by their principal benefactor, Mrs. Gertrude Clark Whittall, an infirm octogenarian dowager who was nearly deaf. It was a common occurrence that just before the musicians were ready to sound their first note, a loud comment arose from Mrs. Whittall, who was obviously oblivious of the silence in the room prior to the first sound of music. The musicians, as well as most of the regular audience, knew the source of the disturbance. They smiled, relaxed for a moment, then resumed their concentration and commenced playing. It was almost an expected routine of the recitals.

I remember these concerts as almost unique in giving the ultimate in musical satisfaction. In the course of the series, the quartet covered the canon of classical and romantic chamber music literature but also ventured into twentieth century music, playing the Bartok quartets and music by Schönberg, Berg, and contemporary composers.

The Juilliard Quartet often included other artists in their concerts, outstanding among them were the pianists Claudio Arrau, Leon Fleischer, Lucas Foss, and Beveridge Webster, the violist Walter

Trampler, the cellist Leslie Parnas, and the clarinetist Harold Wright.

For the first time we were also able to enjoy opera in Washington. The Opera Society of Washington, under the direction of Paul Callaway, gave several good performances, usually without top artists, yet with some notable singers of international reputation. During 1962–1964 we heard six performances: Richard Strauss's *Ariadne auf Naxos* with Reri Grist and George Shirley; Mozart's *Cosi fan tutte* with Elaine Bonazzi, Patricia Brooks, George Shirley, and John Reardon; Rossini's *Barber of Seville* with Hermann Prey, Donald Gramm, and Loren Driscoll; Puccini's *Gianni Schicchi* and Ravel's *L'Enfant et les Sortileges,* again with Reardon, Bonazzi, and Brooks; Mozart's *Die Entfuehrung aus dem Serail* with David Lloyd and Donald Gramm; and Puccini's *Madama Butterfly.*

On a trip to Eastern Europe, I stopped in Vienna and had the opportunity to attend a terrific performance of Richard Strauss's *Ariadne auf Naxos* with Evelyn Lear singing the part of the composer and Leonie Rysanek as Ariadne, and two operettas at the Volksoper, *The Merry Widow* and *Die Fledermaus,* both with a sprightly soprano, Adele Leigh, who until then had been unknown to me.

Back in Washington, we had a delightful reunion with Roberta Peters in 1962. Accompanied by George Trovillo, also an old friend from their Soviet tour, and the flutist Samuel Pratt, she sang a recital of compositions by Handel, Donizetti, Debussy, Meyerbeer, and Johann Strauss. Peters returned to Washington in 1964 to sing in a National Symphony concert under Howard Mitchell.

We did not subscribe to the National Symphony during those years, primarily because we were able to attend concerts by some of the major U.S. orchestras that came to Washington yearly. The New York Philharmonic came twice in 1963, giving us a chance for reunions with Leonard Bernstein and his musicians. In the first concert they played Mendelsohn's Symphony no. 4, Debussy's *Iberia,* and, the pièce de résistance, the trio from the last act of Richard Strauss's *Der Rosenkavalier* with the wonderful Phyllis Curtin, Judith Raskin, and Regina Sarfati. In the second concert, the young pianist Andre Watts played Liszt's Concerto no. 1, while the orchestra played Schumann's Symphony no. 3 and Stravinsky's *Firebird Suite.*

The Philadelphia Orchestra came to Washington in 1964, our first hearing of that renowned ensemble and another reunion, this time with Georg Solti. They played Beethoven's Symphony no. 6 and Stravinsky's *Sacre de Printemps,* one of Gyuri Solti's specialties.

In 1964, on their return from a successful tour in the Soviet Union, the Cleveland Orchestra, under the great George Szell, played in

Washington. Their program consisted of Haydn's Symphony no. 31, Henry Dutilleux's *Metaboles,* and Beethoven's Symphony no. 3.

Finally, we attended a concert by the Berlin Philharmonic in 1965, conducted by its music director, Herbert von Karajan. It was only my second time hearing this by now world renowned conductor since that performance of *Fidelio* at the Berlin Staatsoper in September 1938. They played Beethoven's Symphony no. 6 and Richard Strauss's *Ein Heldenleben.*

I mentioned earlier that Ed Murrow, for whom I was working, became a role model for me. During his directorship, the United States Information Agency came into its own, both within the U.S. government and around the world. Renowned as the epitome of journalistic professionalism, this most prestigious of American broadcast journalists brought to the job an unmatched reputation for integrity and honesty. Merely through his presence, Murrow lent the agency a new level of acceptance within the bureaucracy. Not only was he an accomplished practitioner of public diplomacy, he embodied it. Throughout his life he was the great communicator who, through his personality, his integrity, and his skill as a conveyor of information, inspired confidence in the truthfulness of his message.

Murrow's thoughts on public diplomacy were best articulated in an interview with Edward P. Morgan, another respected Washington journalist. Morgan quotes Murrow as saying in that interview: "It has always seemed to me the real art in this business is not so much moving information or guidance or policy five or ten thousand miles. That is an electronic problem. The real art is to move it the last three feet in face-to-face conversation."

Murrow thought of public diplomacy as an art—the art of getting the message from the loudspeaker to the mind of the foreign listener, or from the book into the consciousness of the foreign reader. And the importance he attributed to personal contact, the direct relationship between the purveyor of information and his target, resonated throughout my career.

On one occasion, Murrow called me on a Saturday morning and asked me to come down to the office to brief Danny Kaye, who was about to travel to the Soviet Union under the auspices of the U.S.-Soviet Cultural Agreement. In the course of the briefing, I admitted to Danny (as he immediately identified himself) that I had always envied him in one respect, namely that he could get in front of any orchestra and "conduct" to his heart's desire!

After the meeting, Danny invited us to go to lunch, suggesting that we fly to Philadelphia in his private plane and eat at Bookbinders.

Ed and I demurred, and we settled on a nearby restaurant. As the three of us ambled down Pennsylvania Avenue, I noticed people stopping in their tracks and staring as they immediately recognized those two famous characters. I turned to Murrow and suggested that they must have been asking themselves, "Who are those two guys walking on either side of Tom Tuch?"

On the professional side, I saw Ed Murrow really angry only once, and that was when the Soviets unilaterally broke the informal 1958 moratorium on atmospheric nuclear testing. His reaction to the news was one of unmitigated fury. He called us into his office, instructed the Voice of America to mass its transmitters, and announced that he would write and personally air a commentary, denouncing the action as "a crime against humanity" and severely detrimental to the U.S.-Soviet relationship. And he did.

Ed Murrow resigned from USIA in 1964. He died of lung cancer in 1965. As long as I knew him I had never seen him without a Camel cigarette between his fingers. His successor, Carl Rowan, was a former Minneapolis newspaper journalist who had joined the Kennedy administration as ambassador to Finland and then as an assistant secretary of state. It was a new ball game, as far as I was concerned, and I went into intensive Polish language training, planning to assign myself to Warsaw as public affairs counselor, where I would succeed my close friend, Wallace W. "Pic" Littell. Rowan, however, wouldn't let me go, insisting I remain in Washington for another year in the same position I had held under Murrow.

In March 1965, I resumed studying Polish, hoping to finally make it to Warsaw that summer. Again, fate in the form of the new USIA director, Leonard Marks, interfered. A prominent communications lawyer close to President Johnson and his family, Marks wanted to bring about a closer integration between the Department of State and USIA. As one measure, he offered me a job I couldn't refuse: as deputy chief mission (DCM) at the U.S. legation in Sofia, Bulgaria.

So, back in State for the third time, I stopped studying Polish on a Friday and started intensive study of Bulgarian on Monday, which lasted for two weeks before departing for my next post and managing to keep our original reservations on the U.S.S. *Constitution.* (On the ship we struck up a friendship with the family of Christopher van Hollen, who was en route to Ankara, like me as a DCM. One of their kids, Chris Jr., now represents the Maryland suburbs in Congress and chairs the Democratic Congressional Campaign Committee.)

5

Bulgaria 1965–1967

In Sofia, my job as deputy chief was to run our mission, which at the time was still a legation, not yet an embassy. There were only two legations left among U.S. diplomatic posts, Sofia and Budapest, whereas all other U.S. missions throughout the world had been raised to embassy status over time. This distinction in diplomatic representation reflected our strained relationship with the Bulgarian Communist regime under the leadership of Todor Zhivkov, which considered itself the Soviet Union's closest ally, almost a satrapy in its Communist orthodoxy and ideological enmity toward the United States.

Most of our American colleagues felt Sofia was the "end station" in the Communist world, citing the fact that it was the final destination for the three Western airlines serving Sofia—Air France, Austrian Airlines, and KLM. Landing at Sofia's dark, primitive airport was indeed a depressing introduction for novices to the Communist world. We therefore made it a practice that as many in our legation as were available—spouses and children included—would greet all new arrivals in order to soften the shock of Sofia landings.

All things are relative, however, and for Mimi and me, whose last post had been Moscow, living in Bulgaria was much easier and pleasanter. For one thing, the climate was less extreme and closer to the European norm. Second, Bulgaria, unlike the vast Soviet Union, was a relatively small country, full of natural beauty—rugged mountains, fertile valleys, and a sunny seashore along the Black Sea coast. The people, although indoctrinated and cowed by their Communist overlords, tried to be friendly and as forthcoming as they could under the circumstances.

Bulgaria was a picture of paradoxes. Sofia, the center of godlessness and antireligious propaganda, sported as its main tourist attraction a golden-domed cathedral, known as the Khramata Alexander Nevsky. During Easter services, the church was so overcrowded with worshippers that it was practically impossible to protect one-self from being crushed during the traditional processions in and around the cathedral's perimeter.

The main square of Sofia sported a huge statue of Russia's Czar Alexander II, known thereabouts as the Czar-Liberator for freeing the Bulgarian nation in 1878 from four hundred years of the "Turkish Yoke." To the best of my knowledge, it is the only statue of a Russian czar anywhere in Eastern Europe.

The main street of Sofia, running the length of the city, was paved with yellow wooden bricks, causing tourists driving into the city on a rainy wet pavement to slide every which way, colliding with local vehicles. (In the interest of full disclosure, the only souvenir that I carried with me from Bulgaria was one of these yellow wooden bricks that I surreptitiously dug up late one night before leaving the city. There was only one factory left that manufactured these bricks, and it was in Budapest, a remnant of the splendor of the Austro-Hungarian empire.)

In contrast to the Russians, who would aggressively defend themselves against any criticism of their society, the Bulgarians had a national excuse for anything that didn't work. When reminded, for instance, that the elevator in our nine-story apartment building had been "under repair" for a week, they would shrug their shoulders and respond: "Remember, Mr. Tuch, four hundred years of the Turkish yoke!"

My boss, the American minister, Nathaniel Davis (who became a close friend), unfortunately had to depart from the post prematurely in the spring of 1966, leaving me as chargé of the legation, pending the appointment of Jack McSweeney as the new chief of mission. McSweeney, however, delayed his arrival for several months to await the raising of the legation to embassy status so that he could be an ambassador rather than a minister.

The small Western diplomatic corps was a friendly and rather tightly knit group owing to its isolation from the embassies closely associated with Moscow. We entertained each other frequently and thought up various pretenses to have parties—à la Lawrence Durrell, who described in his delightful classic *Esprit de Corps* the diplomatic life in post–World War II Belgrade.

Together with Derek Thomas, the British DCM and my closest friend in Sofia, I organized one such party, a scavenger hunt. Teams of guests—all Western diplomats and their wives—were instructed to find clues all over Sofia and race to be the first to identify and locate them all. It was quite a sight, seeing carloads of diplomats careening all over the city, followed by their "tails," who must have become utterly confused as to whom to follow when the diplomats' cars suddenly stopped, their passengers jumped out, exchanged vehicles, and raced off in different directions. The perplexed submachine gun–armed militia guarding the palace of the Communist party headquarters in the center of Sofia watched bunches of foreigners racing up to the building, jumping out, and counting the number of windows on the imposing structure. The next morning, both Derek and I were called to the Protocol Section of the Foreign Ministry and admonished for our undiplomatic behavior.

The major crisis during my term of office came about on June 6, 1967, the day after what became known as the Six-Day War broke out in the Middle East.[8] By way of background, Todor Zhivkov and his Communist cohorts routinely exhibited their loyalty to Moscow by organizing "spontaneous" anti-American demonstrations in front of the American legation building. Those of us who worked there were not surprised by these protests because someone from the Bulgarian Foreign Ministry would call and give us two hours warning so that we could remove our cars from the street outside. This would save the Bulgarians precious dollars in reparations that they might have had to pay if the demonstrators destroyed American cars. Having moved our cars, we would wait for the demonstrators, many of whom had been gathered through repeated radio announcements over the state radio encouraging the protest against dastardly American capitalists for one alleged inimical policy or another. Once assembled, the crowd shouted insults and threw rocks at the legation, usually breaking most of the windows in the four-story brick office building. Trapped inside, the staff hunkered down under desks until the demonstrators dispersed. Then the minister or I would rush over to the Bulgarian Foreign Ministry to lodge a stiff protest. The Bulgarians would reject the protest on the grounds that the demonstration had simply been an expression of disapproval by democratic Bulgarian forces, often even insisting that they had protected the legation from more drastic action by the aroused Bulgarian populace. After this pro-forma denial, the Bulgarians would grudgingly agree to repair the legation building. The next day they would send glaziers and carpenters to do the work.

Accustomed to this semi-violent Cold War routine, the legation was taken by surprise on that June 6, when a real demonstration developed, incited by the news that war had broken out in the Middle East. Engulfed by nationalist spirit and wanting to show Arab solidarity, Syrian students—not Bulgarians—headed for the Israeli legation; but when they were turned away by a phalanx of Bulgarian police, they veered to the nearby unprotected American legation. The students locked the legation's single Bulgarian militia guard in his booth and proceeded to wreak havoc. They torched cars parked in front of the building, threw paving stones and bricks through windows and tried to rush the building. The legation's cultural attaché, John Clayton, who happened to be near the entrance, shut the security door at the last moment, preventing an invasion but suffering a blow on the head for his vigilance.

While this was happening, I was in my second floor office, which faced the street and the demonstrators. With rocks and glass flying around me, I clutched my telephone and ducked under my desk for safety. From this perch, I frantically called the Bulgarian police, fire department, and Foreign Ministry to appeal for help. Between calls, I glanced out a broken window in time to see my personal car, a 1965 Ford station wagon, explode in flames.

After fire trucks had extinguished the fires and police had driven back the demonstrators, we emerged from our hiding places to assess the damage, especially that done to our devastated personal and legation-owned vehicles. Five cars, including mine, had been completely destroyed, and seven had been damaged. This would be the first time we would claim reparations from the Bulgarian government for anything as costly as American cars, and we would be making our claim in hard currency. We knew that there would be considerable opposition from the Foreign Ministry when I told them the bill would be $50,000.

As I drove to the ministry, I decided to go to the American section instead of the protocol section where we would normally present our bill. The head of the American section was a former Bulgarian ambassador to the United States and one of the few Bulgarian diplomats familiar with the American way of doing business, so I knew he would understand the offer I was about to make. I told him that instead of claiming dollars, we would accept leva, the Bulgarian currency that was worthless outside the country, for the sum owed us, as long as there would be no argument about the amount. He was incredulous. "Do you mean leva, not dollars?" he asked. When I said I did, he replied, "Will you shake hands on the deal?"

Having shaken my hand, he disappeared for ten minutes and returned with a stack of leva that looked as fresh as if they had just been printed in the basement. Before we parted, he happily assured me that all repairs to the legation would be undertaken immediately. Having no doubt anticipated haggling over the amount of a dollar payment, he could now expect compliments from his superiors for having saved the ministry valuable hard currency.

After I returned to the legation, I consulted with the administrative staff to determine who was owed damages and in what amounts. Since the legation needed the leva for its operating expenses and would normally have to exchange dollars for them at the Finance Ministry, we paid the Americans in available dollars and reserved the leva for the embassy's expenses. Almost everyone was happy: the car owners were reimbursed in dollars and the Foreign Ministry did not have to forfeit its scarce hard currency. A minor diplomatic and financial crisis had been avoided, with only two losers: the Bulgarian Finance Ministry, where probably no one knew why the American legation did not purchase its monthly allotment of Bulgarian leva, and the Syrian students. Annoyed that the student demonstration had cost them unplanned reimbursements to the Americans, the Bulgarian Foreign Ministry declared that it would not permit outsiders to preempt the conduct of its foreign affairs and the next day dispatched all sixty of them home to Syria.

On the larger diplomatic stage, Bulgaria also broke relations with Israel and declared the Israeli minister *persona non grata*. When this happened, the Italian ambassador suggested calling our NATO colleagues to tell them of the Israeli minister's departure, and propose that they come to the airport to bid him farewell as a gesture of friendship. When I called my diplomatic colleagues to give them the time of his departure, to my surprise several claimed that they did not have "instructions" from their governments on the matter. I replied that one hardly needed instructions to say good-bye to a friend, and added that they might not receive invitations for the usual Sunday night movie showings in our family apartment if I didn't see them at the airport. That evening, when the Israeli minister departed, there was a full complement of friendly diplomats and spouses to bid farewell to the minister and his family. We also hosted an unusually large crowd the following Sunday night when we screened a Western with beer, coke, and popcorn.

After this lengthy exposition on life and work in the American legation, the reader might think that during our two years in Sofia there was no music. Wrong. One of our great surprises upon arrival in Sofia was to discover that there was not only an opera house but a very good one, with a long and still active performance tradition. Productions, especially of the Russian repertory, were often excellent, even superior in some instances to what we had heard at the Bolshoi in Moscow. We witnessed top-notch performances of Mussorgsky's *Boris Godunov* (with Nicolai Ghiaurov) and *Khovanchina* (with Nicolai Gyuselev and Dimiter Petkov), Borodin's *Prince Igor* (with Nicolai Gyuselev) and Tchaikovsky's *Pique Dame*, and lesser but still substantial productions of the Italian repertory, and even an occasional novelty, such as Rameau's *Les Indes Gallantes*. Altogether we attended seventeen performances at the Sofia Opera. (Some of my diplomatic colleagues slanderously claimed that since the Opera heated its building in the fall before the central heating came on in our apartment building, we found an inexpensive refuge there from the cold.)

The one Bulgarian export industry that, in my opinion, could compete successfully on the world market was operatic bassos, produced with almost Five-Year Plan precision. After the great Boris Christoff in the 1950s came the equally great Nicolai Ghiaurov, then the fine Nicolai Gyuselev and the young Dimiter Petkov, who won the grand prize in the 1967 Sofia opera competition.

Nicolai Ghiaurov returned to Sofia yearly during our time there and was hailed as a triumphant hero after conquering the international opera stage. The Sofia Opera, intent on capitalizing on their star's drawing power, forced all those who wanted to hear the basso sing in his hometown to buy subscriptions to seven performances, in only one of which Ghiaurov would sing. Since, however, the top price for seats at that time was two levas (or $1 at the official exchange rate), the entire subscription cost only $7 — not bad for hearing Ghiaurov's Boris.

We did manage to hear Ghiaurov not only in *Boris Godunov* but also twice as King Philip in Verdi's *Don Carlo* and once in a concert with the Sofia Philharmonic, singing excerpts from *Khovanchina* and *Boris Godunov*. At the time he was at the apex of his distinguished singing career.

One musical high point of our stay in Sofia was the quadrennial international competition of opera singers in the spring of 1967, especially so since there were American participants for the first time, and there was one American judge on the panel. He was the noted American baritone, John Brownlee, then the director of the Manhattan School of Music. We welcomed him and became friends during the two weeks he spent in Sofia. I remembered hearing him in many Met broadcasts in the 1940s, especially as the Count in The *Marriage of Figaro* and in the many Verdi baritone roles.

The surprise of the competition was a young American mezzo soprano, Joy Davidson, who won the gold medal over her Russian competitor. The latter had been expected to win in light of the prevailing political situation in Bulgaria at the time, as reflected in the makeup of the panel of judges. But in this instance, excellence won out over politics! Joy sang the aria "O don fatale" from Verdi's *Don Carlo* in her "victory" concert, bringing forth a standing ovation and ten minutes of rhythmic clapping in the Sofia opera house.To even things out politically, as expected, a Russian tenor won the men's division, while the young Bulgarian basso, Dimiter Petkov, won the overall grand prize.

6

Berlin 1967–1970

Returning to Berlin after ten years' absence—a second homecoming for me—was a real shock, both physical and sociological. The most important, most visible, and certainly most tragic was the Wall that now divided Berlin into two cities, in two different and unfriendly countries. Since its erection in 1961, the Wall had by 1967 become a political, economic, social, and cultural, if emotionally unacceptable, reality that Berliners had learned to live with. Thus, one could no longer talk about *Berlin's* cultural life; it was West Berlin's and East Berlin's cultural life, and the twain rarely met.

Beyond that, and equally critical for an American diplomat concerned with human relationships, the close friendship between Berliners and their American partners had severely deteriorated. Whereas most Berliners continued to feel safe and grateful in the presence of the Americans as their only protectors against the Soviet threat, an active and vocal minority of mostly young people had turned against the United States and what it stood for in the world.

Many in the previous generation of Germans had, rightly or wrongly, considered the United States their Camelot; now, a significant number of the so-called "successor generation" opposed America for a variety of reasons. Certainly, U.S. involvement in Vietnam, the upheavals of the civil rights revolution in America, the assassinations of John F. Kennedy, Bobby Kennedy, and Martin Luther King contributed to a conviction that America was no longer a model society but the enemy of society.

Beyond that, German youth were suffering from a growing anxiety about the world in which they lived. Among the components of this angst were:

— fear of war, especially nuclear destruction;
— environmental concerns;

— alienation in a highly industrial society consisting of large impersonal organizations, including government;
— the problems of unemployment in this harsher world with a shrinking social net;
— bad conscience over being part of an affluent society while millions in the Third World starved; and
— an absence of national identity, a consequence of living in a divided country that had been defeated and destroyed in a terrible war.

This radicalization of young Germans often turned violent in Berlin, with frequent destructive demonstrations against the America House, the American cultural center, Berlin's most visible manifestation of the United States. Lectures and discussions on American policies and social issues were often broken up violently. On several occasions when, as head of the U.S. public diplomacy mission, I was invited to deliver a lecture or participate in a discussion at the Free University or other public institution, my appearance on the podium would be greeted with a barrage of tomatoes, eggs, and worse, so that I had to be escorted out of harm's way by the police, without ever having uttered a word.

One example of this precarious situation involved a performance of *Tannhäuser* at the Deutsche Oper. Mimi and I had anticipated this evening because Jessye Norman, the young American dramatic soprano, was making her debut in the opera house in the leading role of Elisabet. She had hardly finished her first aria, "*Dich teure Halle*," when there was a loud interruption on the public address system: "We have an emergency. Is a Mr. Tuch in the audience?" We both jumped up—while the music continued—making our way from the middle of the first row in the balcony to the aisle to be met by two policemen, who informed us that a bomb had been found in the America House.

By the time we reached the America House in the police car, the bomb squad was removing the bomb, which had only partially exploded and caused a fire in the cloakroom. Unfortunately, we did not hear the end of Jessye Norman's performance that night.

Anti-Americanism, coupled with the then-fashionable anti-establishment attitude prevalent among the city's radicalized young people, found an outlet in the Deutsche Oper. No premiere of a new production took place without a cacophony of boos, whistles, cheers, shouting demonstrations, and even fisticuffs between those who were against the establishment (and the American participants in it) and those who rose to the defense of order and legitimate artistic expression. Artistry, or the lack of it, had little to do with it.

There were moments of such real physical and emotional tension that my wife, for one, decided not to attend premiere performances after one particularly unpleasant incident that occurred during a new production of Strauss's *Ariadne auf Naxos*. Evelyn Lear, one of Berlin's most admired and popular American singers, was booed vociferously when she took her curtain call after the Prologue, for no apparent artistic reason. This, as she told me later, disconcerted the young American soprano, Cathy Gayer, who still faced the fiendishly difficult Zerbinetta aria of the following act. Right in the middle of her acceptably executed coloratura passage, someone in the audience yelled, "*Das reicht ja nicht für Kottbus*" (the equivalent of someone shouting at the Met, "That ain't good enough for Newark"), and pandemonium ensued.

On any other evening, without the political claque in the theater, both singers would be cheered by those who appreciated them as artists regardless of their nationality. Loren Maazel, the opera's music director, learned to handle such disturbances. Once, after he was booed when he ascended the podium for the second act of an opera performance, he turned around and in perfect German announced: "Those of you who didn't like the first act might as well go home now because I assure you the second act will be much worse." This was part of opera life in West Berlin in the late 1960s.

A welcome relief from the unrelenting anti-American atmosphere came on October 13, 1969, with the visit to Berlin of Neil Armstrong, Michael Collins, and Edwin Aldrin, the three astronauts who had recently landed on the moon. They received a tumultuous popular reception.

Being the public affairs officer of the U.S. mission in Berlin, I was fortunate to become thoroughly acquainted with the Deutsche Oper company, with the people who ran it, and with the performers who contributed to making it the distinguished institution it was at that time. Between 1967 and 1970 I attended forty-six Deutsche Oper performances. It is not an easy task to review these three seasons without becoming mired in a swamp of detail. I will begin with some general comments.

Deutsche Oper

The Deutsche Oper was run by two outstanding personalities: Gustav Rudolf Sellner, the *Intendant* (General Manager), was a man of long and distinguished experience in the theater; Lorin Maazel, the music director, though not yet 40, was a musician and conductor of highest reputation and worldwide renown. Maazel combined musicianship, taste, and technical command of his craft

American Astronauts Neil Armstrong, Edwin Aldrin, and Michael Collins (with author in the background) upon their arrival at Berlin's Tempelhof airport, October 1969 (U.S. Information Service).

with an intellectual and artistic breadth that found few peers in contemporary musical life. The two men infused in the company a high degree of sophistication, intelligence, artistry, and operatic joy.

Evidence that good music-making was the predominant impulse in the Deutsche Oper of the late sixties was, first, the quality of the conductors under contract to the house, notably, Karl Böhm, Eugen Jochum, Joseph Krips, Christoph v. Dohnani, Giuseppe Patane, Bruno Maderna, the choral director Walter Hagen-Groll, and Lorin Maazel—not just as occasional guest performers, but as conductors engaged to prepare and lead new productions in the repertory. Second, singers were engaged for ensemble productions for the entire season—not just for the first two or three performances of a new production—and they were of high caliber. To name just a few demonstrates this point: Fiorenza Cossotto, Helga Dernesch, Hilde Gueden, Gundula Janowitz, Sena Jurinac, Catarina Ligenza, Erika Köth, Pilar Lorengar, Edith Mathis, Leonie Rysanek, Carlo Cossutta, Jose van Dam, Ernst Häfliger, Gianni Raimondi, Martti Tavela, and Ingvar Wixell.

American singers constituted a third pillar of qualitative support for the Deutsch Oper. A disproportionately large number of American artists were engaged as soloists during that period. I counted fifteen, all of whom made a substantial contribution to the repertory and some of whom enjoyed world recognition. Among them were artists such as Evelyn Lear, Thomas Stewart, James King, Annabelle Bernard, Catherine Gayer (who became the opera's leading coloratura soprano), Jessye Norman, Lee Venora, Tatiana Troyanos, William Dooley, Donald Grobe, and Barry McDaniel.

Maazel's pivotal position at the opera was by no means the principal reason for the apparent tilt toward American artists. I talked to him and to Sellner about this. They reasoned that these American singers were just plain good, superior to other artists in a competitive environment. Maazel, who became a good friend, did not, to the best of my knowledge, form personal relationships or maintain social contact with any of his American singers. He explained that American vocal artists were expertly trained in American conservatories and universities, better than those in similar institutions in Europe. But though these Americans were well prepared vocally, dramatically, and, above all, musically, in the United States they had relatively little opportunity in those days—we are speaking of the 1960s—to get practical operatic experience and gain a reputation performing. In Europe they could get both, first in provincial opera houses and later in the international ensembles in Munich, Vienna, Frankfurt, Hamburg, and Berlin. These international casts also made it possible—indeed, dictated—that operas would be sung in their original language rather than in German translation.

Among the successful new productions we heard were Verdi's *Simon Boccanegra* (Maazel, Sellner: Janowitz, Wixell, Talvela, van Dam, Sardi, Cossutta); Verdi's *Otello* (Maazel, Sellner: Charles Craig, Jurinac, Giuseppi Taddei); Strauss's *Der Rosenkavalier* (Krips, Sellner: Rysanek, Troyanos, Mathis, Franz Mazura, Cossutta); Alban Berg's *Lulu* (Böhm, Sellner: Lear—later Gayer—Patricia Johnson, Fischer-Dieskau, Loren Driscoll, Grobe, Greindl); Tchaikovsky's *Pique Dame* (Martin Turnovsky, Oscar Fritz Schuh: Bernard, Johnson); Puccini's *Tosca* (Maazel, Boleslag Barlog: Lorengar, Tito Gobbi).

Lest this list give the impression that the Deutsche Oper limited itself to productions of the classic repertory, I list here some of the novelties, old and new, that created considerable interest and excitement for the opera-going public. I should add, however, that unlike the major opera companies in the United States, which are often criticized for their conservatism and lack of initiative in bringing new works to the stage and showcasing contemporary composers, the Deutsche Oper and the many other civic and state-operated opera companies throughout Germany are heavily subsidized by local and state governments, in some cases up to 60 percent for each ticket sold. Thus they can afford to experiment and not fear bankruptcy when they face evenings with unsold tickets because of public disinterest in their esoteric offerings.

Among these often scintillating novelties were Carl Orff's *Catulli Carmina* and *Carmina Burana*, Cimarosa's *Il Matrimonio Secreto*, Schoenberg's *Moses und Aron*, Berg's *Wozzek*, Luigi Dallapiccola's *Odysseus*, Richard Strauss's *Capriccio*, and Boris Blacher's *200,000 Taler*.

What stood out at the Deutsche Oper during that period, in comparison with other opera companies, were consistently good performances. The opera shone not only on its premiere evenings but also at subscription performances night after night. It was, for instance, a real pleasure to attend the 70th performance of a *Figaro* production just to hear Elisabet Grümmer, Edith Mathis, Catherine Gayer, William Dooley, and Gerd Feldhoff; or the 41st performance of *Rigoletto* to hear Hilde Gueden, Giacomo Aragall, and Ingvar Wixell; or the 138th evening of *Cosi fan tutte* to hear Eugen Jochum conduct Teresa Zylis-Gara, Kersten Meyer, Lee Venora, Luigi Alva, Barry McDaniel, and Ivan Sardi in a still fresh and refreshing ensemble performance.

Yes, there was the occasional downside. One new production of Rossini's *Cenerentola* just did not sparkle as it should have; *Un Ballo in Maschera* had gotten too dusty and tattered to deserve repetition for the 155th time. One learned to avoid evenings where a certain *Taktschlager* (time beater) with too long a tenure in the company was at the podium. But these were exceptions. I venture the judgment that in overall excellence the Deutsche Oper shone brighter than its German and most of its European competitors during that period.

Completing the picture of the West Berlin opera scene were two visiting opera companies: Georg Solti's London Royal Opera in 1970, with Verdi's *Falstaff* (Geraint Evans, Regina Reznik, et al.) and *Don Carlo* (Carlo Cossutta, Gwynneth Jones, Josephine Veasey, et al.); and the Stuttgart State Opera the same year, with two interesting, seldom-heard operas, Krzystof Penderecki's *The Devils of Loudon* (Janos Kulka, Colette Lorand, Richard Holm, et al.) and Brecht/Weil's *Rise and Fall of the City of Mahagony* (Harry Pleva: Martha Moedi, Anja Silja, et al.).

East Berlin

In East Berlin, the Staatsoper on Unter Den Linden had been restored to its old splendor, architecturally if not musically. A second East

Berlin opera house, the Komische Oper, which eclipsed it artistically, was virtually the private domain of Walter Felsenstein, the almost legendary opera producer/director, among whose disciples were the likes of Sarah Caldwell and Goetz Friedrich.

As an American diplomat in Berlin, I was in the fortunate position of being among the few with easy access to East Berlin. I was thus able to visit both opera houses, although it was not always easy to manage attendance because there was no telephone communication between the two cities. One or two visits to the Staatsoper convinced me that what one got to hear and see was not worth the difficulty of getting schedules and tickets for performances. This was a formidable task necessitating at least two personal trips to East Berlin, changing currency, and facing other bureaucratic difficulties, such as finding the box office closed for no explicable reason, or learning that attendance at performances was restricted and that programs had been changed without prior announcement.

Once these barriers had been overcome, one found oneself in a splendidly reconstructed baroque auditorium, but what one heard and saw was mediocre at best."Provincial" performances, such as one of Mozart's *Entfuehrunq aus dem Seraglio,* sufficed to discourage further efforts to obtain tickets. The one exception I noted was the excellent tenor Peter Schreier, who appeared to divide his time between East and West Germany.

It was entirely different at the Komische Oper, Felsenstein's preserve. Mimi and I became friends of the Felsensteins, a colorful family in an otherwise drab and largely humorless society. They were flamboyant in every respect: the imperious, straight-backed, serious *pater familiae;* his gregarious, ostentatious, almost "kooky" film-making wife, Maria; their two sons, one an actor who preferred to live in West Berlin, the other his father's assistant. They were not bound by the confines, austerity, and mediocrity of East Berlin's normal lifestyle. They had an apartment in West Berlin and a baronial estate in Glienicke, just outside East Berlin, complete with stable, three-car garage, heated outdoor swimming pool, and a huge kitchen, equipped entirely with the latest General Electric utilities and gadgets.

They owned two Mercedes cars and a late-model Ford stationwagon, the latter decorated on its rear window with an American flag and decals from various American states they had visited. Felsenstein had all the perks of a highly privileged East German Communist Party official (except for the fact that he and his wife also managed to travel on Austrian passports). He also apparently enjoyed a practically unlimited budget for his opera house.

I first met Felsenstein when I arranged a visit to his opera house for Leonard Bernstein in September 1968. Bernstein was in Berlin with the New York Philharmonic and wanted to pay a call on the famous director as well as see one of his productions. We attended a performance of *La Traviata* during which Lenny, in his usual uninhibited manner, made disparaging noises in criticism of the musical execution of the opera. The conducting and singing were indeed sluggish. But all of us were fascinated by the staging, the way the chorus moved around the candle-lit drawing room in the first act as though individually directed. It was realism at its most dramatic.

Afterwards, we spent some time with Felsenstein and his elder son, and they invited me to come back. This contact, later to develop into friendship, eliminated for me my earlier difficulties of securing tickets for performances at the Komische Oper. It still took some doing because of the absence of direct telephone connection between East and West Berlin. The way we overcame that hurdle was by my calling a colleague in Vienna who, in turn, would call Felsenstein's office in East Berlin to relay my request for tickets for a given performance.

Thus we were able to view some ten productions, all the ones Felsenstein wanted us to attend, plus a couple directed by his protégé, Goetz Friedrich, who later served many years as *Intendant* of the Deutsche Oper in West Berlin. Among the Felsenstein productions we saw were Benjamin Britten's *Midsummer Night's Dream*, Prokofiev's *Love for Three Oranges*, Offenbach's *Tales of Hoffmann*, and *Bluebeard*. We also attended Friedrich's productions of Leos Janacek's *Jenufa* and Richard Stauss's *Salome*, as well as a way-out production of the way-out Hans Werner Henze's *Der Junge Lord*.

These operas did provide a more interesting and eclectic fare than that offered elsewhere in Europe. What made them entirely different from other opera productions I had seen is signaled by the fact that whereas heretofore I wrote primarily about the musical personalities involved in opera presentations, here I name exclusively the stage directors—Felsenstein and Friedrich.

What made Felsenstein different, in my mind, is that he cared primarily about the dramatic side of opera—how productions would look and feel and project as theater—and only secondarily how it would sound as music. In that respect, he was the precursor of some of his contemporary imitators—Ponnelle and Zeferelli, to name just the two most conspicuous—who appear to have dominated the opera stages in Europe and the United States with their visual extravaganzas.

Unlike some of them, however, Felsenstein would not try to alter the spirit, dramatic sense, or story line that the composer had intended. He believed in what the Germans call *Gesammtkunstwerk*, the combination of drama, music, scenery, and costumes in the creation of a total opera concept; but his method and vision gave priority to the drama over the music, as exemplified in all of his productions I witnessed and in the gigantic film of Verdi's *Otello* that he produced and directed.

Felsenstein was so involved with the psychological and visual aspects of an opera that he could not help but deemphasize the musical composition. For one thing, he had the freedom and resources to spend months in the production process and rehearsal—often as long as six to eight months—before he would permit an opera to be performed for the public. Thus, he could retain few first-class artists for that long a period of time to do his creative bidding. Second, in any artistic difference with the music director of a production, it was clear that he, the master, would prevail. Thus, his conductors tended to be less important personalities in the creation of a new production than might be required to do justice to the composition. One was therefore always fascinated by the imagination, insight, and visual aspects of a Felsenstein production and sometimes disappointed in the quality of the music one heard. Nevertheless, Felsenstein's stature and importance as a creative force and inspiration to others is secure in any contemporary history of opera.

More Music in Berlin

As professionally difficult and often frustrating as my three years in Berlin were in the late sixties, musically they were the richest and most illuminating in my lifetime up to that point. Having reported on the opera scene, I now turn to record the concerts and recitals in Berlin from 1967 to 1970, which I hope will not cause the reader's eyes to glaze over as I list the orchestras, conductors, and soloists. Nor do I want to give the impression of mere name dropping. One caveat: I am not a critic and thus not qualified to analyze or criticize the performances. My memory of most of these concerts is based on impressions, intuition, personal prejudices, and experience in listening.

During those three years, Mimi and I attended thirty-nine concerts of the Berlin Philharmonic, eight of them conducted by its musical director, Herbert von Karajan; seventeen concerts by the Berlin Radio Symphony Orchestra, ten of them conducted by its musical director, Lorin Maazel; concerts in Berlin by six other top orchestras ; and twenty significant concerts and recitals by various choirs, chamber music groups, and individual musicians.

I start with conductors. Karajan was clearly a great conductor, and his orchestra was one of the world's finest. (Among the many wonderful musicians occupying principal chairs in the orchestra at the time was James Galway as principal flutist.) I have always been somewhat conflicted about Karajan's conducting, based obviously on personal taste rather than objective critical judgment. For instance, in one concert he conducted the third act of *Götterdämmerung*, and I remember that evening to this day. He and his soloists, Helge Brioth, Helga Dernisch, Karl Riddenbusch, Gerd Neustedt, and Christine Hetzell, created a totally satisfying musical drama without benefit of scenery, costumes, or lighting.

On another evening, he conducted Dvořák's cello concerto with Mstislav Rostopovich, achieving complete rapport between conductor, soloist, and orchestra that resulted in magical music making. And there was also an inspiring, quite deliberate, yet beautiful reading of Beethoven's Ninth with Gundula Janowitz, Christa Ludwing, Jess Thomas, and Walter Berry.

Less to my amateur taste was Karajan's reading of Bruckner's Symphonies no. 8 and 9 and a ponderous and idiosyncratic performance of Beethoven's Symphony no. 3; while Bartok's *Music for Strings, Percussion and Celesta* was done with zest and precision that showed off the perfection of the orchestra.

I never met Karajan. Wolfgang Stresemann, the *Intendant* (administrative director) of the orchestra, and I were friends, and I showed him the 1938 program of the *Fidelio* performance (when Karajan made his Berlin Staatsoper debut). Stresemann, who was writing a biography of Karajan, let him see the program. Karajan didn't have a copy of it, Stresemann told me, and wanted to keep it, but I made him a photocopy instead.[9] I should note that thanks to Stresemann's hospitality, we were able to sit in the *Intendant's* box on the many occasions we attended concerts in the Philharmonic.

An amusing incident occurred when Leonard Bernstein and the New York Philharmonic came to town in September 1968 to participate in the annual Berlin Cultural Festival, and it was suggested that Bernstein and Karajan meet. Since Karajan never attended other conductors' concerts, it was arranged that during intermission he would come to the concert hall, known popularly as Karajan's Temple, for a brief meeting in Bernstein's dressing room.

The meeting took place, and afterwards, when I asked Lenny how it went, he replied "I don't know. He asked me how I liked the hall, and I responded that I really couldn't tell yet, since this was our first concert and we had played only the Haydn [Symphony no. 87]." Early the next morning, I received a phone call from Heinrich Keilholz, the acoustic engineer who had been responsible for the concert hall's acoustics when it was built. Keilholz told me that he had just had an urgent call from Karajan instructing him "Do something about the hall. Bernstein doesn't like the sound!"

Many memorable concerts by the Berlin Philharmonic took place under other conductors, and it would be difficult to name them all. I do, however, want to report on some outstanding ones, starting with George Szell, who, I was told, came almost every year to conduct the Berlin Philharmonic. We met Szell and his wife in 1967 at a small dinner party. During a conversation about which were the greatest concert halls in the world, I ventured that I thought I knew two of them. Szell, noticing me for the first time, asked abruptly, "Which ones?" I said, "The Concertgebouw in Amsterdam and the Leningrad Symphony." He barked, "And the third?" When I replied that I could name only two. He shot back, "Severance Hall [in Cleveland] of course!"

Later he asked whether my wife and I were coming to his concert the next night. I said of course, and he suggested having supper afterwards. The concert was great, featuring the Haydn Symphony no. 93 and the Bruckner Symphony no. 3, the Bruckner a new and deeply moving experience for us. As we emerged from the concert hall, he asked whether we could recommend a typical Berlin place with good beer. I suggested our favorite *Kneipe* (beer joint), Hardtke, where one ate and drank at long, rough wooden tables and benches. The dish Hardtke was famous for was *Eisbein mit Sauerkraut und Erbsenpuree* (pigs knuckles with sauerkraut and split pea purée), washed down by a liter of beer.

Apparently it hit the spot. Szell started out with three *Steinhegers* (Schnaps) in quick succession, followed by a beer chaser. Not only did he then eat the lean inner meat of the pigs knuckles but also tackled the fat around it, adding the rest of his wife's plate plus another liter of beer. I thought to myself that the aged conductor was never going to make it until morning, and that I would have him on my conscience. Not so. The next morning he called and said that we would have to repeat that the next year.

And so we did. Most reports I have read about George Szell describe him as the severe, autocratic disciplinarian before whom everyone quaked. For Mimi and me, he was an expansive, pleasant food and drink enthusiast with a lively sense of humor, but then, I was not a member of his famed band. On that score, he held that his Cleveland Orchestra was the best in the world, but he did allow that the Berlin Philharmonic had the finest bass section he had encountered.

Among the outstanding conductors we heard with the Berlin Philharmonic were William Steinberg (Stravinsky violin concerto with concertmaster Leon Spiers); Thomas Schippers with Byron Janis playing the Prokofiev Third Piano Concerto, and on another occasion playing Strauss's *Ein Heldenleben*; and Sir John Barbirolli conducting the Mahler Fifth and Clifford Curzon playing Mozart's piano concerto in D Major (K. 537 "Coronation"). On another occasion, Sir John conducted a fantastic Verdi *Requiem*; on still another occasion he conducted the Sibelius Fifth Symphony and Gina Bachauer playing the Beethoven Piano Concerto no. 3; and on a final occasion, Sir John conducted the Brahms Symphony no. 3 and Christoph Eschenbach playing the Beethoven Piano Concerto no. 2.

Karl Böhm conducted Mozart's Symphonies nos. 39, 40 and 41, and, on another occasion, Beethoven's Third Symphony and Webern's *Passacaglia*. Zubin Mehta led the Philharmonic in Dvořák's Cello Concerto with Jacqueline Du Pré; Carlo Maria Giulini conducted Schubert's Symphony no. 4 and Debussy's *La Mer*; Claudio Abbado conducted Stravinsky's *Oedipus Rex*; Seiji Ozawa conducted Glazunov's Violin Concerto with Michael Schwalbe; Juri Temirkanov led Mozart's Piano Concerto (K. 414) with Malcolm Frager; Aaron Copland conducted his own Symphony no. 3; Moshe Atzman conducted the Prokofiev Cello Concerto with Paul Tortelier; Ernest Ansermet conducted the orchestra in Honegger's *Jeanne d'Arc au bucher*; and Wolfgang Sawallisch conducted Beethoven's Symphone no. 6 and Mozart's Piano Concerto no. 19 (K. 459) with Christoph Eschenbach.

Several visiting orchestras also performed in Berlin during our stay there. I already mentioned the New York Philharmonic in 1968 with Leonard Bernstein performing Mahler's Fifth Symphony, one of Lenny's favorites. (As he came off the stage, sweating and exhilarated, he announced "I never realized that this piece was so Jewish!") His other program consisted of William Schuman's Third Symphony and Berlioz's Symphonie Fantastique.

The Los Angeles Symphony under Zubin Mehta played Beethoven's Third Symphony and Andre Watts performed Liszt's First Piano Concerto. The American minister, Brewster Morris, my boss, and his wife Ellen enjoyed entertaining American artists and did so frequently and graciously. Andre Watts was among those we became acquainted with at the Morrises, The successful young American pianist had come to play with the Los Angeles

Leonard Bernstein, the author, and the Governing Mayor of Berlin, Klaus Schütz, in conversation at a reception after the concert of the New York Philharmonic in Berlin, September 1968 (U.S. Information Service).

Philharmonic but also performed with the Berlin Philharmonic and gave a much acclaimed solo recital.

The Cincinnati Symphony Orchestra played one concert under Max Rudolf and a second under Erich Kunzel, with the jazz pianist David Brubeck performing music by Bernstein, William Schuman, and Brubeck. George Solti came twice, once with the New Philharmonia Orchestra (Brahms no. 2) and once with the London Philharmonic Orchestra (Mozart no. 25, Bartok Dance Suite, and Beethoven no. 5). Another fine orchestra that we had not heard before was the Residenz Orchestra den Haag under Bruno Maderna, playing an interesting program by Debussy, Nicolas Nabokov, Anton Webern, and Pierre Boulez.

Our attendance at Berlin Radio Symphony concerts might constitute a separate chapter in our Berlin story. Although somewhat in the shadow of the blockbuster Berlin Philharmonic, the Radio Symphony was, by anyone's standard, a fine ensemble, enjoying a first-class reputation not only in Germany but throughout Europe. We had already attended a few of the concerts, conducted by its music director Lorin Maazel and featuring such well known pianists as Friedrich Gulda, Rudolf Firkusny, and Julius Katchen when Byron Janis came to Berlin to play with the orchestra.

We had known Janis from his appearance in Moscow in 1959, so I called him and suggested supper after his concert. (We also knew his wife, Maria, since we had met her as a teenager in Moscow when she accompanied her parents, Gary Cooper and his wife, to the Moscow Film Festival in 1960.)

On the day of the concert, Byron called to ask whether we would mind if Lorin Maazel joined us for supper. We, of course, readily agreed. The concert went well—Janis played Rachmaninoff's Rhapsody on a Theme of Paganini, and Maazel conducted Beethoven's Third Symphony—and we proceeded to Aben, one of our favorite local restaurants,. We had met Maazel on a couple of occasions, but this was our first real acquaintance with him. During dinner it developed that although Janis and Maazel had seen each other over the years, this was the first time they had played together since the night in Pittsburgh in 1943 when the 12-year old Maazel conducted and the 14-year old Janis performed with the Pittsburgh Symphony Orchestra.

We learned from Byron that Vladimir Horowitz, who had given a recital in Pittsburgh the night before, was persuaded to stay over to hear the young Janis play. And, after the concert, Janis told us, Horowitz asked him to become his student. He added that he was the only student Horowitz ever taught.

We subsequently attended all of Maazel's concerts with the Radio Symphony. They were always of a high caliber and sometimes had fascinating programs, such as Robert Schumann's *Das Paradies und die Peri* with the excellent soloists Annabelle Bernard, Anna Reynolds, Donald Grobe, and Keith Engen.

One concert we especially remembered featured the young Israeli pianist Israela Margalit playing the profound Brahms First Piano Concerto. Subsequently we regularly met Israela in Lorin's company. One evening Lorin called to invite us to his nearby house, and I queried the occasion of this sudden invitation. Lorin replied that Israela and he had just come back from Mexico, where they had been married, and wanted us to help them celebrate their nuptials. We did so in the company of one other couple, and in between bottles of champagne, Lorin even got out his fiddle and entertained us.

We enjoyed our relationship with Israela and Lorin and saw each other frequently in Berlin and subsequently whenever our paths crossed. Lorin and I used to have long conversations, but I can't remember any where music was discussed. Politics, German-American relations, or social issues were our subjects. It is possible that what drew us together was my ignorance about his field of expertise and his about mine—neither of us was a threat or had to compete in the profession of the other.

I know that some people found it difficult to relate to Lorin. I attribute that to a certain shyness or reticence, perhaps in part because this child prodigy never had a normal childhood, and throughout his youth people were awed by his talent and intelligence, to which he reacted negatively. I was aware that he did not have personal relationships with the artists at the Deutsche Oper, including the Americans. They respected him as an artist but had no social contact with him. Mimi and I found him a warm person, made even warmer through the influence of his effervescent wife, Israela. Years later, after their divorce, we stayed in touch mainly with Israela, primarily because she came to Germany often while we were stationed in Bonn, pursuing her career as pianist.

I don't want to leave our Berlin years without briefly mentioning a few more outstanding musical events. RIAS (Radio in the American Sector), the radio network operated by the U.S. government and broadcasting primarily to the Communist Zone of Germany, sponsored a series of three concerts per year called "RIAS Stellt vor" ("RIAS Introduces"), presenting young talent to the music world in orchestral concerts. Among those featured was Jessye Norman in one of her first public performances.

And finally, among the memorable recitalists we heard were Andre Watts (twice), the Italian mezzo soprano Teresa Berganza, the American pianist Gary Graffman, the American violist (and close personal friend) Rafael Hillyer, the Juilliard Quartet, the New York Pro Musica (under Noel Greenberg), and, at the America House, the German baritone Herbert Brauer, Jessye Norman, the American pianist Ann Schein, and the American cembalist Virginia Pleasants.

With Richard Nixon in Ireland

Exchanging once more my musical cap for my public diplomacy helmet, I want to commit to history my involvement with President Nixon's "trivial junket" to Ireland in 1970.[10] It was a purely political trip in line with the obligatory pilgrimages presidents and presidential candidates make to Italy, Ireland, and Israel to cement support from these important constituencies. In this case, a principal White House goal was to recall Mr. Nixon's purported Irish ancestry through the Milhous family connection.

Since the U.S. embassy in Dublin had no USIS representation, I was asked to come from Berlin and, together with my colleague,

Stan Zuckerman from Brussels, assist the presidential advance team in arranging the public aspects of the visit, which turned out to be the *only* reason for the trip. It was one of those instances where public diplomacy was misused for purely political purposes. To this day the episode sticks in my craw, though it did have some humorous aspects.

The visit started out badly with the arrogant and bad-mannered behavior of the White House advance team that arrived in Dublin ostensibly to plan the trip with the Irish government but, in effect, proceeded to dictate the itinerary to their Irish interlocutors. I cringed at their crude and insensitive attitude, exemplified by their response to the Irish deputy foreign minister's gentle suggestion that it would be appropriate to have President Nixon call on the president of Ireland and the *Taoiseach*, as the Irish prime minister is called.

"Why?" asked a White House advance man.

The Irish official replied that it was a courtesy and proper protocol to have a visiting head of state call on the top officials of a country.

"How long a visit?" came the question.

"I'd suggest one half hour each," the deputy foreign minister replied.

"We'll give them no more than twenty minutes" came the definitive response!

The first stop on the president's itinerary was Limerick on the West coast, where one of Mr. Nixon's patrons named Mulcahy owned a castle at which he hosted the president. With little news to report, my friend Max Frankel, the *New York Times* White House correspondent, sent his dispatch to the paper in the form of a twelve-stanza limerick over which he labored prodigiously for several hours. With his permission, two of the stanzas are reproduced here:

> He stayed in a millionaire's house—
> Mulcahy, who often shoots grouse.
> But the hunt on this day
> Was for much bigger prey:
> "A kingdom for just one Milhous.

> "Don't care how he spells it," he said.
> "Or whether he's living or dead.
> "I need a relation
> "In this mighty nation
> "Lest the polls once again drift to Ted."

To Max's disgust, word came back from his editors in New York that the *Times* does not publish such frivolous material.

As the limerick spells it out, one purpose of the trip was to legitimate Nixon's supposed Irish roots through the Milhous connection, and I was assigned to find the cemetery where the Milhous ancestors were alleged to be resting in peace. It was going to be one of the stops on the president's itinerary.

I knew that this was going to be difficult, since the Milhous clan were apparently Quakers who buried their dead in informal burial places, not designated cemeteries. I borrowed a U.S. Army helicopter and flew in the general direction of a place called Timahoe, where the burial place was supposed to be. I landed on several farms and asked the farmers for directions. None of them knew, but they gave me contradictory instructions on which direction to turn. After bobbing down and up in my helicopter for about forty-five minutes in a fruitless search, I made an executive decision and designated a peaceful, tree-lined grove as the Quaker burial place housing the Milhous remains. It became the designated stop for a brief presidential visit and photo-op.

The next morning, alas, the *Irish Times*, a Dublin morning newspaper, had an anonymously sourced front-page story: American diplomats were sent out to find President Nixon's ancestral burial place, and they found it. But when they assembled a number of broken stones, low and behold, the inscription on the gravestones spelled K-E-N-N-E-D-Y! The White House advance party was not amused.

We left Berlin in November 1970, musically sated and looking forward to a new public diplomacy experience—far from the Communist world with which we had been involved for thirteen years. Brazil was to be our next assignment, with Portuguese a new language that we had not encountered before.

7

Brazil 1971–1975

Before embarking for Rio, we spent four months in Washington, cooped up in a temporary apartment and studying Portuguese intensively. Our son David was in college at Grinnell and our daughter Andrea, age 16, was farmed out to Mimi's sister on Long Island so that she would not miss a whole semester of high school.

Studying Portuguese was difficult, especially for two people, not particularly gifted linguistically, who had been involved with German and the Slavic languages for many years. Most important, we were in our mid-forties, an age at which, my experience demonstrated, one's ability to learn a new language deteriorates.

Furthermore, Mimi and I discovered that intensively studying a language together with one instructor tended to impede an otherwise happy marriage. Luckily, the period of scholastic rivalry and mutual linguistic recrimination lasted only twelve weeks and ended before permanent marital damage developed!

Two short trips to New York to see our daughter and enjoy some music helped relieve the linguistic tension. We managed to see an outstanding opera performance on each visit. One was a Met performance of *Fidelio*, conducted by Karl Böhm. Featuring Caterina Ligenza in the title role and Helge Brilioth as Florestan, the production also included Edith Mathis, William Dooley, Murray Dickey, and Paul Plishka. The next time we saw the by-now-famous New York City Opera production of Boito's *Mephistofele*, conducted by Julius Rudel and featuring the legendary Norman Treigel in the title role, a performance that certainly justified its fame. Gilda Cruz-Roma sang Marguerite.

In mid-March 1971, we were off to Brazil. We had originally booked passage on the Moore-MacCormack passenger ship *Brazil*, hoping for a leisurely ocean voyage to Rio de Janeiro. Unfortunately, Moore-MacCormac took its two passenger vessels, the *Brazil* and the *Argentina*, out of commission two weeks before our scheduled departure. So, we decided on the only alternative, a Moore-MacCormack freighter that took only twelve passengers, three of whom were Mimi, our daughter Andrea, and I. It was a leisurely two-week voyage, with only one stop—in Savannah, Georgia. We continued our Portuguese language study in between dips in the freighter's 15'x12' so-called swimming pool.

Life in Brazil was an entirely new proposition that did not, however, include opera and but little classical music. Compensating was the constant beat of samba music, the beach, and the ocean!

The process of transferring the capital of Brazil from Rio de Janeiro to Brasilia was just picking up steam in 1971, and the American embassy was among the first to heed the Brazilian government's insistence on moving to the new capital. Brasilia was a political, economic, and social necessity for such a huge country. Eighty percent of Brazil's population reportedly lived within 100 miles of the Atlantic coast. In order to open up the country to development and population, the capital had to move inland (reminiscent of the need to establish Washington as the capital of the United States 200 years earlier). Planned and built largely by the city planner Lucio Costa and the renowned architect Oscar Niemeyer, Brasilia in the early 1970s when we lived there was a monument to sterile modernism, dedicated to the machine—the automobile—devoid of the humanity of normal city life. The best description of Brasilia that I heard was that it was like the World's Fair the night after it closed; but I won't go into detail about Brasilia's shortcomings in 1971. Thirty-seven years later, Brasilia had become a working and living capital. When we lived there, it was in its infancy, populated by the government, its ministries, and civil servants and, in several adjacent unplanned satellite communities, the working people who made the city run. Our cook, a culinary artist, refused to move to Brasilia with us. Her explanation: *"Não tem escinas en Brasilia"* ("There are no corners in Brasilia"), meaning there are no street corners where friends could meet in the evening for casual conversation. And, indeed, there were few sidewalks in Brasilia because everyone seemed concentrated on transportation by car or bus.

Since my work involved institutions that were still located primarily in Rio—the media, publishing houses, cultural entities, universities—I was permitted to retain an apartment in Rio, where I spent three days a week, while maintaining our principal residence in Brasilia. This semi-separation was tough on Mimi, who remained in Brasilia with Andrea, then spending her last year in high school in the newly created Brasilia American high school.

Because of the size of the country and its federal character, USIS Brazil had nine branch posts ranging from Belem in the north to Porto Alegre in the south—a six-hour plane ride between them—and including such major metropolises as Rio de Janeiro, São Paulo, Belo Horizonte, Salvador Bahia, and Recife. (USIS São Paulo itself, because of that city's importance as an economic, communication, and intellectual center, had a staff of five American officers, the equivalent of a medium-size country post.) Not only did I spend much time shuttling between Brasilia and Rio, I also did a lot of traveling to the other branch posts in order to maintain a cohesive program, secured by agreed public diplomacy objectives.[11]

During my last year in Brazil, Ambassador John Hugh Crimmins, a man I greatly admired, asked me to be deputy chief of mission (DCM)—again, a request I couldn't refuse—so my deputy, Fred Coffey, largely ran the USIS show.

Back to music, during our four years in Brazil, we attended only one opera performance, a special production of *Rigoletto* in the ornate Rio opera house. We attended the event because of the guest appearance of Cornell McNeil in the title role. We had never heard him before, and, to be honest, my only recollection of the performance is his superb characterization of the role and that great voice.

One musical highlight of our stay in Brazil was the tour of the Cleveland Orchestra under Lorin Maazel. They performed in Rio and São Paulo under USIS auspices, playing Samuel Barber's *School for Scandal* Overture, Bartok's *Magnificent Mandarin Suite* and the Brahms First Symphony. The Brazilian public were ecstatic over this fine orchestra. For Mimi and me it was also fun to spend a week with Israela and Lorin.

Another U.S. orchestra that visited Rio in 1973 was the Utah Symphony under its long-time conductor, Maurice Abravanel. I had never heard this orchestra before, and I was much impressed by their performance, especially by their sensitive playing of the Mozart Symphony no. 35 and the Brahms First Symphony, as well as Villa Lobos's "The Little Train of the Caipira" from *Bachianas Brasilieras*, which particularly pleased Brazilian listeners.

In respect for Mormon tradition Mimi had arranged for plenty of extra ginger ale and fruit juice for the members of the orchestra at our after-concert reception . We were surprised—and amused—when the thirsty musicians requested mostly scotch and bourbon.

The U.S. and several other foreign diplomatic missions in Brasilia contributed to the celebration of the sesquicentennial of Brazilian independence in 1972 with art exhibitions and performing arts groups (the latter limited in size by the availability of appropriate performance space). I had heard that Andre Watts, the young American pianist whom we had befriended in Berlin in the 1960s, was planning performances in Latin America, so I contacted his agent and arranged for a Watts recital in Brasilia at a reasonable special fee.

An unanticipated problem arose when we had difficulty finding a decent concert grand for him to play in the movie theater we had rented for the concert. We finally found what we thought was an acceptable piano, but it was badly out of tune. Twenty minutes before the start of the concert, there was Andre in shirtsleeves lying under the piano wrestling with the instrument, trying to get it into tune. He had to repeat the chore during intermission. Yet, it was an outstanding recital: he played Schubert's op. 143, Beethoven's Sonata no. 23, and Chopin's Sonata no. 2. The audience wouldn't let him go until he had played several encores, and until the piano was about to give out for good.

On the way to the airport the next morning I asked Andre where I should send the check with the fee. He asked me what we were supposed to pay, and I told him his agent had agreed to the very low fee of $1,000. He turned to me and said, "Tom, after all the U.S. government has done for me, I can't accept any money for this recital." I argued with him but to no avail. I finally insisted on remunerating him at least for his travel expenses for which I subsequently sent him a check. It was never cashed. Andre Watts was not only one of his generation's finest musicians but a wonderful guy!

We were able to bring several other American artists to Brasilia, among them the pianist Gary Graffman, the New York Pro Musica under Noel Greenberg, and the violist Rafael Hillyer, our close friend. Rafe, who had by this time left the Juilliard Quartet, played recitals and conducted master classes in Rio and São Paulo. He also played recitals in Brasilia and Goiania, the provincial capital of the state of Goias, where no American artist had ever performed. Goiania received him as a conquering hero, a reception that a violist, even as fine a one as Rafe, does not normally encounter.

One nonmusical experience that reverberates in my memory was the visit of James Michener, who came under the auspices of the USIA American Specialist program to "communicate" with Brazilian audiences. Michener turned out to be the ideal communicator. He had a way of creating empathy with interlocutors so that they would talk about issues and themselves in a nonconfrontational atmosphere. I told him I feared that my own conversations with him would find themselves into one of his books, where I would evolve into one of his characters.

Andre Watts, with Mimi, at our house for dinner after his concert in Brasilia , 1972 (H. N. Tuch).

People, especially young people and students, were drawn to his engaging and friendly personality, and he would involve them in discussions on a variety of issues that interested him, such as civil rights, race relations, and cultural diversity. I accompanied him to Rio and São Paulo to meet with university faculty and students and other young people. At the end of a week's tour, I asked him whether he would like to get together with one of his old friends, the famed actress and musical comedy star, Mary Martin, and her husband Richard Halliday, who lived part of the year on their *fazenda* (farm) in Anapolis, about 80 miles west of Brasilia. The friendship of Mary Martin and Michener dated back 25 years to when she played Nellie Forbush in *South Pacific*, which was based on Michener's *Tales of the South Pacific*. Michener jumped at the chance, and Mary was delighted to have us come out and spend the night.

I should explain here that Mary and her husband had purchased the *fazenda* years earlier as a recreational getaway home, at the suggestion of their close friends, actress Janet Gaynor and her husband Adrian, the famed film costume designer, who owned an adjoining property. (Both Gaynor and Adrian were no longer alive when we were in Brazil.) While the Hallidays' property was a working farm with cattle and fowl, Richard had designed the residential area into a lovely rustic vacation complex, complete with a Japanese garden and small waterfall. Kerosene lanterns and candles, lit by local household servants, illuminated their house and adjoining guest cottage.

Richard excused himself after dinner because of a bad cold. Mary and Jim then engaged in a two-hour conversation as they caught up on each other's life and activities, while I mostly just listened. The gossip and reminiscences about Broadway friends and nonfriends— some pretty sharply drawn—wafted about in the balmy evening air of our somewhat incongruous Brazilian surroundings.

In the nearby town of Anapolis, Richard Halliday had designed and built for Mary Martin a charming boutique where Mary sold her famous needlepoint creations along with fashions and jewelry by Brazilian designers. And next door to the shop, Richard had created a chic beauty parlor, straight from Fifth Avenue, staffed by local nuns, all named Maria (after a character in you-know-what musical). Embassy wives occasionally journeyed to Anapolis to shop in Mary's boutique and have lunch with her. Mary and Richard also came to Brasilia from time to time to attend embassy parties.

What Brazil lacked in opera it made up in the quantity and quality of its contemporary artists, in particular one incomparable writer, Jorge Amado. The author of such colorful, expressive, and evocative novels as *Gabriela, Clove and Cinnamon,* and *Donna Flor and Her Two Husbands,* he was the beloved godfather of the natives of Salvador da Bahia, the most colorful and richly historic city in Brazil. We were able to get to know this delightful man and his wife through our USIS

James Michener and the author visiting Mary Martin at her fazenda near Anapolis in the Brazilian state of Goias, 1974 (Graham French).

branch public affairs officer, Frances Switt, who was Miss America incarnate in Salvador. Having lived there for a dozen years, she knew everyone in Bahia (as Salvador da Bahia is known in Brazil) and had close friendships with Jorge Amado and many artists.

The fine printmaker Calasans Neto (who physically resembled Toulouse-Lautrec) was her close friend and became ours as well. We own a nunber of his works on paper and on wood. Other artists we got to know whose works we acquired included the German-born but totally Brazilian Hansen-Bahia, as well as Emanuel Araujo, Caribé, Glenio Biancetti, Faiga Ostrower, Maria Bonomi, and Carlos Scliar.

Before leaving Brazil, I should mention several more outstanding musicians and musical groups we were delighted to hear in Brasilia: the Brazilian pianists Nelson Freire and Jacques Klein, the string quartet of the Portland Symphony, the Pro-Musica Cologne, the English Chamber Orchestra under the conductor John Pritchard, the Pro Arte Quartet, the Chamber Orchestra of Salzburg, the American violinist Erick Friedman, the American pianists Thomas McIntosh and Joel Rosen, the Quarteto Beethoven de Roma, and the Soni Ventorum of the University of Washington. Nearly all the non-Brazilian musicians were presented under the auspices of their respective embassies.

Several of my friends, as I mentioned earlier, have always claimed that I never accepted assignment to a foreign post that lacked an opera house. My four years in Brasilia prove otherwise. Visiting the opera house in Manaus doesn't count, since there hadn't been any performances there since the turn of the century. This remarkable structure on the Amazon River, recently restored to its former glory, was in dire disrepair when I first visited Manaus in 1971. It had been built in the 1890s in ostentatious baroque splendor by the Brazilian rubber barons who literally ruled the Amazon basin at the time and lived a life of luxury incongruous with the impenetrable jungle that surrounded them. Over the ensuing years, after the world rubber market collapsed, the famous opera house fell victim to neglect and the encroaching jungle, and appeared like a mystic ruin of a bygone era.[12]

8

Back in the USA 1976–1981

Fletcher

After ten years abroad, I spent my next assignment, on sabbatical, as the Edward R. Murrow Fellow and visiting professor at the Fletcher School of Law and Diplomacy at Tufts University in Medford, Massachusetts. The Murrow fellowship had been established in memory of the legendary news correspondent and director of the U.S. Information Agency (USIA) during the Kennedy administration, for whom, as noted earlier, I had worked. It was indeed a change of pace. My only responsibility was to prepare and teach a course in public diplomacy and to advise and consult with graduate students interested in or planning a career in the Foreign Service.

Evidence of the "small world" theory was the presence in my Fletcher seminar of a singularly committed student named David Welsh. Nearly twenty years earlier, in 1957, the five-year-old David had been the inseparable playmate of our four-year-old daughter Andy, when the Welsh and Tuch families were immediate neighbors while serving at the American Consulate General in Munich. David is today a distinguished Foreign Service officer, serving since 2005 as assistant secretary of state for Near Eastern Affairs and no doubt practicing quite a bit of public diplomacy.

We found an apartment in what I called Watergate North, a huge luxury complex in nearby Malden. It was 1976, the year of the bicentennial, and we took full advantage of all the commemorative exhibitions and depictions of historical events in the Boston area. This city was new to us, as was the whole of New England, which we enthusiastically explored during the year.

Musically there were a number of outstanding events. Through my connection with the Boston Symphony twenty five years earlier, I was able to secure a hard-to-get seven-concert subscription that enabled us to reacquaint ourselves with that fine orchestra. Seiji Ozawa, the orchestra's music director, conducted four concerts, one of them particularly memorable, Berlioz's *Romeo et Juliet* with the soloists Julia Hamari, Jean Dupony, and Jose van Dam. Another outstanding concert Ozawa conducted featured Dvořák's Cello Concerto played by the wonderful Mstislav Rostropovich, an old acquaintance from our Moscow days.

Colin Davis conducted one of the subscription concerts, featuring Sibelius's Sixth Symphony and Mendelsohn's *Incidental Music to a Midsummer Night's Dream*; Michael Tilson Thomas conducted Mahler's Ninth Symphony; and Andrew Davis led the orchestra in Michael Tippett's *Ritual Dances* and Elgar's Second Symphony.

Opera was limited to one outstanding performance by the Boston Opera Company under Sarah Caldwell. It was particularly interesting to hear her, knowing that she had studied under Walter Felsenstein with whom we had been friendly in Berlin. The opera was Verdi's *Macbeth,* with Ryan Edwards in the title role, and Shirley Verrett as Lady Macbeth. Varrett was a veritable vocal harridan—terrific in both voice and characterization.

Our close friends Rose Marie and Henry Dunlap visited us from Washington, and together we drove up to Tanglewood to hear a concert by the Boston Symphony, under the baton of two conductors. Seiji Ozawa conducted Tchaikovsky's *Serenade for Strings*; then Gunther Schuller conducted his own *Symphonic Tribute to Duke Ellington*; and Ozawa ended the concert with Tchaikovsky's *1812 Overture.*

Mimi and I made one brief trip to New York and spent the evening with our friend Rafael Hillyer and his wife Kyoko (who herself had become a successful concert impresario). Together we crossed the street from their apartment to Lincoln Center to hear the New York Philharmonic under Leonard Bernstein (we were his guests) play Copland's *An October Overture*, deFalla's *El amor brujo*, and, the pièce de résistance, Bernstein's *Four Songs*, with the soloists Victoria Canale, Elaine Bonazzi, Florence Quivar, and John Reardon.

Before leaving Boston, I must relate an experience that involved a certain amount of chutzpah on my part. I received a call from the manager of the Cleveland Orchestra inviting me to give a preconcert lecture at the orchestra's summer venue, the huge amphitheater at Blossom, near Cleveland. I knew the manager, Kenneth Haas, from my earlier contact with the orchestra, but I suspected Lorin Maazel of instigating the invitation. (Lorin later swore that he had had nothing to do with it, having been in Europe all summer. To this day I don't believe him.) But, as I said above, chutzpah persuaded me to accept.

The title of the talk was to be "Nothing Short of Perfection: Bringing the Composer's Intent to Its Full Realization in Sound." As purveyors of this subject I named the artists of that evening's concert: Michael Tilson Thomas, the conductor; Itzhak Perlman, the violin soloist; and Daniel Majeske, the orchestra's concert master, who had graciously agreed to demonstrate some of the points I was to make in my presentation. (I had gotten to know Daniel during my previous involvement with the orchestra.)

The spacious amphitheater seemed sparsely attended, but I was told that there were about 5,000 people present at my talk. (The stadium held about 15,000 and it was full for the subsequent concert.) The audience was responsive, thanks largely, I know, to Daniel Majeske's contribution. And it was fun for me, the dilletante with unmitigated gall.

The concert following my talk was delightful: I can't tire of this great orchestra. Under Michael Tilson Thomas it played the Tchaikovsky Symphony no. 4, and Itzhak Perlman showed "nothing short of perfection" in his rendition of the Mendelsohn violin concert

Directing the Voice of America: Washington 1976–1980

My assignment at the Fletcher School was to be for two years but ended prematurely when I was recalled to Washington in October 1976 to become deputy director of the Voice of America (VOA), the worldwide radio broadcasting service of the USIA. After an eleven-year absence we moved back to Washington, where we purchased a house in close-in Bethesda. The house became our permanent home, where we lived until April 2006.

The job at VOA was one of the most fulfilling and demanding of my entire career. Why? VOA was a professional organization of highly qualified radio journalists, engineers, and producers. They took great pride in their responsibility for reliable and authoritative news broadcasts that are, in the words of the VOA Charter, "accurate, objective and comprehensive." That means that no one inside or outside the U.S. government was to interfere with VOA's news broadcasts. As a career officer, not a political appointee, I took it as my responsibility to protect that independence, as mandated by Congress.

Broadcasting in some fifty languages, VOA was the sole source of information from the United States for many people throughout the world, especially those living in the areas of the globe denied free access to the airwaves. It thereby provided an important service in terms of U.S. foreign policy. Managing a diverse workforce of about 1200, furthermore, was a major task, as VOA personnel represented a microcosm of the world in the diversity of their national, ethnic, and linguistic origins. The staff had to be melded into a cohesive team focused on a single mission. For example, the historic differences and conflicts between the Czechs and Slovaks in the Czechoslovak Service, between the Serbs and Croats in the Yugoslav Service, and between old and recent immigrants from the Soviet Union came to the surface frequently and had to be understood and adjudicated.

Finally, as deputy director I had to represent VOA vis-à-vis USIA, its parent organization, the White House (which frequently tried to interfere with VOA's news independence), the Congress (which watched closely over that independence), and the public both at home and abroad. But it was indeed a fascinating job, made more so because during my three years as VOA's deputy director, I had three different politically appointed directors, with long vacancies between them, so that VOA's operations became largely my responsibility, one that I cherished.

Since we are approaching the contemporary era in my musical life, performances and performers I witnessed will be familiar to many readers. I shall therefore limit myself to writing about opera performances, and only about those that, in my view, are historically or creatively significant.

In spite of my heavy and restrictive work schedule, Mimi and I tried to take advantage of the rich musical offerings available in the nation's capital, especially at the Kennedy Center for the Performing Arts. The New York City Opera presented two must-hear productions on their visit to Washington in 1978: Berlioz' *Mephistofele*, conducted by Julius Rudel and featuring Samuel Ramey in the title role, a worthy successor to Norman Treigel whom we had heard earlier; and *The Marriage of Figaro*, also conducted by Julius Rudel and featuring Samuel Ramey, Catherine Malfitano, and Faith Esham.

A performance of Mozart's *Abduction from the Seraglio*, conducted by Reinhard Peters, reintroduced us to the Washington Opera. It was the first time we heard Ashley Putnam.

A novelty was the world premiere of Stephen Douglas Burton's opera, *The Duchess of Malfi*, conducted by Christopher Keene. The production took place in the huge covered "shed" of the Wolf Trap Foundation for the Performing Arts, about ten miles from the city in Northern Virginia. Wolf Trap would become a major attraction for us after my retirement in 1985 and the subject of the last chapter in this book.

During the 1977 season we subscribed to a series of five Brahms concerts by "my" Cleveland Orchestra, all conducted by Lorin Maazel. Besides the four symphonies, Rudolf Firkusny played the piano concerto no. 1, Misha Dichter the piano concerto no. 2, and Isaac Stern the violin concerto. The final concert was the *German Requiem* with the soloists Faye Robinson and Thomas Stewart. All of these concerts persist in my memory as outstanding.

The following year, 1978, we heard the Chicago Symphony under Georg Solti, also doing the Brahms First and Third Symphonies. From his first appearance with the Chicago Symphony in 1954 Solti always considered that orchestra the desired apex of his musical career. During the twenty-two years he headed the orchestra, he molded it in his own image, abetted, by the dedicated musicians of this fantastic ensemble.

Mimi and I met only briefly with Gyuri during that Washington appearance. He introduced us to his new wife, Valerie, whom he had married in 1967. I admit it was a bit of a shock, as we had been so close to Hedi, from whom Gyuri had been divorced. We found Valerie charming and friendly, although we never got to know her, inasmuch as geography and time—and really nothing else—had ruptured our earlier close relationship with Gyuri.

Two outstanding recitals in 1978 stick to my memory. One was a concert by Rudolf Serkin. playing the Beethoven Sonata op. 81 (*"Les Adieux"*) and Schubert's Sonata in B-flat Major (opus Posthumous). This was the last time we heard him. The other recital was that of Itzhak Perlman and Vladimir Ashkenazi playing a Beethoven concert, including the Sonatas op 30, nos. 1 and 3, op. 23 and 24.

In the summer of 1978 we made our first trip to the Santa Fe Opera Festival and took in all four operas in that gorgeous mountain setting. Our first opera was Tchaikovsky's *Eugene Onegin*, conducted by Bruce Ferden. During the first scene, the back of the stage was open, giving us a panoramic view of the Sangre de Cristo mountain range. As the chorus sang while coming home at dusk from harvesting in the field, the sun over the mountains was actually setting in deep red colors, transforming the entire scene into an unforgettable visual and auditory experience. Add to that a fine cast, consisting of Michael Devlin in the title role, Patricia Wells as Tatiana, and Neil Shicoff as Lenski, and you had Santa Fe at its best.

The other three productions were of equal caliber. *Tosca*, conducted by John Crosby, the festival's founder and long-time musical director, featured Clamma Dale in the title role, Jacque

Trussel as Cavaradossi, and Victor Braun as Scarpia; Rossini's *Le Comte Ory*—our first hearing of this charming work—was conducted by Cal Stewart Kellogg and featured John Aler, Sheryl Woods, and David Holloway; and the novelty, the world premiere of—what else?—*The Duchess of Malfi*, this the second opera by that title that we heard within a month. The composer of this *Duchess* was Stephen Oliver; Steuart Bedford conducted the production, Pamela Myers sang the duchess, and William Dooley the evil cardinal. It was one bloody experience, vying in the amount of red stage fluid with the production we had seen at Wolf Trap earlier that summer.

In 1979 we heard a number of notable opera productions in the capital. The Washington Opera presented Massenet's *Cendrillon*, which we had not heard before. Conducted by Mario Bernardi, it featured the great Frederica von Stade as Angelina, a role that along with Rossini's *Cenerentola* she had made her own. With Mimi's understanding, it was love at first sight for me with von Stade, a love that has not dimmed in over twenty-five years. The production featured three other fine women's voices—Ruth Welting, Delia Wallace, and Maureen Forester—plus the noted baritone John Reardon.

We saw the Washington Opera production of Bellini's *I Capuleti ed Montecchi*, also our first hearing of this opera. Conducted by Nicola Rescigno, it featured another great mezzo soprano, Tatiana Troyanos (what is it with me and mezzos?). Her Juliet was Linda Zoghby.

The Kennedy Center sponsored two opera productions that summer in its delightful Terrace Theater, which is acoustically ideal for chamber opera. One was Jacques Offenbach's *Christopher Columbus*, a hilarious concoction made up of the composer's music and a spoof of a libretto. Conducted by Brian Salesky, the cast included Neil Rosenshein, Myra Merritt, Erie Mills, and the incomparable mezzo/comedienne Elaine Bonazzi. The other offering was a double bill of Mozart's *The Impressario* and Carl Maria von Weber's *Abu Hassan*, two youthful trifles conducted by John Mauceri.

A quick business trip to Germany allowed me to reunite with the Deutsche Oper in Berlin. Of the three productions I witnessed, the only pleasurable memory is of hearing Pilar Lorengar and Marti Talvela in a performance of Smetana's *The Bartered Bride*.

On the concert side of the 1979 ledger, we had season tickets for the National Symphony Orchestra, whose musical director was, the great cellist Mstislav Rostropovich. Through Sol Hurok we had become acquainted with Rostropovich in Moscow in 1959, when he was recognized as a musician of world renown but in deep trouble with the Soviet regime. At that time it was not good for him to be in contact with Americans (although he seemed not to care what the authorities thought or did to him). It was great meeting him again under happier circumstances. Ebullient as was his manner with everyone, we were greeted with friendly embraces and kisses.

As a musician—cellist and teacher—Rostropovich, in my view, had no peer since Pablo Casal's death. His playing and his way with students were perfection personified. I share with many the view that orchestral management was, in spite of his knowledge, enthusiasm, and dedication, not his forte. With Russian composers he was obviously at home, but he seemed to lack the interest and technique to build and sustain the orchestra's cohesion and the discipline necessary for producing great music consistently.

We—and the NSO—were exposed that year to other fine conductors, among them Claudio Abbado, conducting Richard Strauss's *Vier Letzte Lieder,* with the great Kiri Te Kanawa (my passions are not confined to mezzos); Antal Dorati, conducting the Mozart Requiem; Christian Badea, conducting the Glazunov Violin Concerto played by Elmar Oliviera; and, in the spring of 1980, Sarah Caldwell, conducting Saint-Saens' Concerto no. 2 and Liszt's Concerto no. 2, with our friend, Andre Watts as the pianist.

Now came a 1979 year-end surprise. On Christmas Eve at around 7 p.m. I received a call from a man who identified himself as Bartolomeo Giamatti, president of Yale University. He apologized for calling so late but said he had chased me all day unsuccessfully (I was preoccupied with VOA coverage of the Tehran hostage situation) and wanted to reach me before the holidays. He explained that a search committee of the Yale Music School had come up with the final two candidates for the vacant position of dean, and that I was one of the two. He wanted to know if I were interested.

I laughed and said, "Dr. Giamatti, you have either the wrong number or the wrong person. I am neither a musicologist nor a musician. I'm obviously the wrong person you want to talk to."

To which he replied, "Mr. Tuch, we do have the right person. By this time we know more about you than you do yourself. We have plenty of musicologists and musicians here. We're looking for someone to run the Music School. Will you come and look?"

I did fly up to New Haven after the first of the year and had a delightful couple of days, meeting a lot of people at the university and the Music School (among them one of my idols, Phyllis Curtin). I had puzzled over how they had found me, and only then did I learn that my good friend, Rafael Hillyer, now teaching at Yale, had been on the search committee. He knew my "record" of involvement with the Boston Symphony, the New York Philharmonic, the New York City Ballet, and the Juillard Quartet tours over the years.

I was, of course, fascinated with this potential career change, but I also recognized that in the end I was unqualified for the job. I learned that one of the dean's principal responsibilities was to raise money for the school. I knew I could not compete in this area with the well-known heads of the other major music schools— William Schuman, Howard Hanson, Peter Mennin—and that I would therefore be unsuccessful. So I went back to Washington, having nonetheless enjoyed the brief encounter with a very fine institution.

The decision to remain in the Foreign Service was not such a difficult one, because I now looked forward to my dream assignment as Minister Counselor for Public Affairs in Germany—the head of the largest USIS mission in the world. Before our next move, however, we attended two memorable opera performances in the spring of 1980. One was the Washington Opera's *Tristan and Isolde*, our first live hearing of this work. Julius Rudel conducted and Spas Wencoff and Roberta Knie sang the title roles, with Hanna Schwarz as Brangäne, John Macurdy as King Mark, and Norman Bailey as Kurvenal.

The other cherished performance of that spring was the Met's production of Verdi's *Un Ballo in Maschera* at the Kennedy Center. It is to this day Mimi's favorite opera, and it was a particularly fine production. Conducted by Michelangelo Veltri, it featured Luciano Pavarotti—at the peak of his vocal career at that time—Gilda Cruz Roma, Louis Quilico, Judith Blegen, and Bianca Berini. It was a great finale to our Washington assignment.

9

Bonn 1980–1985

In the summer of 1980 we were transferred to Bonn. I had been promoted to the rank of Career Minister in 1975, the highest in the Foreign Service, except for the rarely attained Career Ambassador. Given a choice of being appointed ambassador to a small East European or African country or becoming Minister Counselor for Public Affairs in Germany, I decidedly preferred the latter. This, for me, was the pinnacle of my career. I spoke German (Mimi did also); I knew the country and its people; I had a large professional staff and a budget to serve our objectives in the country; and I believed I could succeed in this post, which turned out to be my last before retirement.

Heading the USIS establishment in the Federal Republic of Germany (FRG) from 1980 to 1985 was a fascinating job, albeit more complicated and difficult than expected. Although the FRG was a close ally and intimate partner of the United States politically and economically, major changes within the German society had taken place that complicated the US-FRG relationship. Many young Germans, dissatisfied with their own society and particularly with their foreign policy vis-à-vis the Communist East, took their frustration out against the U.S. presence in their country, with anti-American demonstrations and sometimes violent activities.[13]

We concentrated our public diplomacy program on bridging the gap in understanding, especially between the young people of our two countries—the so-called Successor Generation. An example of the several projects we undertook to reconnect our two societies was a conference in Berlin in April 1982 of young American and German national and regional legislators.

Steny Hoyer, then a young Maryland congressman, now the Democrats' majority leader, headed the American delegation.

Other participants were members of the state legislatures in California, Texas, New York, North Carolina, Ilinois, Colorado, New Hampshire, Kansas, Pennsylvania, and Georgia. They and their German counterparts met for three days of dialogue with distinguished German and American officials, intellectuals, and politicians, among them Richard von Weizsacker, the then governing mayor of Berlin, and later president of the Federal Republic of Germany.

For both the American and German participants, normally concerned with local or regional issues in their respective countries, the formal sessions and, even more, the informal conversations were stimulating and eye-opening, producing relationships that led to subsequent contacts and exchanges.

Arthur Burns

The appointment of Arthur Burns as U.S. ambassador to Bonn in the spring of 1981 contributed substantially to making my assignment a real pleasure. Dr. Burns was known throughout the world as an economist, teacher, central banker, and counselor to presidents, in the last instance to Ronald Reagan. He quickly realized that in order to fulfill his responsibilities, he would have to study and learn—about diplomacy, about foreign affairs, and about Germany. He assigned his senior staff—the deputy chief of mission, me, the economic counselor, and one or two others—to perform this task, and we did so in a number of seminars that became detailed discussions of foreign policy and diplomatic practice.

Dr. Burns announced early on that he planned to give several public speeches and asked for help, emphasizing, however, that preparing his speeches would take four to five weeks. I told him that I would be unable to assist him since I could not take that much time from my other duties.

Some weeks later he asked for suggested topics for his first major speech. I mentioned that I thought an appropriate subject might be, "How America Looks at Europe." He replied that he understood that I would be unable to assist him with his speech writing. I said that if he agreed to the subject I had suggested, I would be glad to help him. And so a relationship developed in that I would do the first draft, he would consider it, ask tons of questions, critique every aspect of the draft, and then polish it to his own style. (Later on I became familiar with his style, so the process became smoother and faster, except for the questions that his unfortunate aide had to research and answer satisfactorily—often fifteen pages of questions for a twenty-page speech.)

He gave his first speech on the suggested subject in Bonn before a distinguished academic and political audience, and to my amazement it was published in full not only in most major German newspapers, but also in the *Wall Street Jounal* and, in an abridged version, *Reader's Digest*.

I quickly concluded that the time it took helping Ambassador Burns with his speeches was well spent; if I wrote a speech for myself and gave it before, say, the Chamber of Commerce in Stuttgart, there might be ninety people in attendance and the text might be covered in the two local newspapers. But a speech written for Ambassador Burns, I discovered, would receive wide international recognition that I could never achieve with anything authored under my own name.

As a result, I worked with Dr. Burns on all of his subsequent speeches except those on economic subjects, recognizing that I knew next to nothing about economics. However, he made me edit all of his speeches. On one occasion, I objected to a certain paragraph in an economic speech, telling him that it made no sense to me. He immediately retorted, "That's because you're stupid." I agreed but pointed out to him that many in his audience would probably be as stupid as I am and not understand it either. He insisted that he was not going to change anything, so I left. Fifteen minutes later he called and asked me politely to come back. When we were seated across from one another, he pushed his draft over to me and gently said, "Fix it." I told him I couldn't fix it because I didn't understand what he was talking about, whereupon he asked his secretary not to disturb him and gave me an absolutely clear forty-five-minute lecture on the subject of my ignorance. I then understood and was able to "fix" his speech. We developed a warm relationship, both professional and personal.

Dr. Burns decided that his main contribution as U.S. ambassador to the FRG should be to communicate with the young Germans of the Successor Generation. He did so brilliantly, hosting frequent private sessions—with only Mrs. Burns and himself present—over tea with university students of all stripes. The students, while perhaps initially suspicious, were obviously flattered by his attention.

He continued to give public speeches dealing with issues of consequence and interest to German audiences, who flocked to his lectures.[14] Even at my age of 59, I considered Arthur Burns a mentor. Unexpectedly returning the favor, he told an audience at a farewell dinner for Mimi and me upon our departure from Germany in 1985 that he, at the age of eighty, had found a mentor in me. No more flattering if undeserved statement had ever been made about me, and that is why I unashamedly repeat it here.

Here I am going to digress for a moment to describe the most embarrassing moment in my Foreign Service career. It occurred in December 1982 and involved Secretary of State George Shultz.

What under another secretary of state would very likely have been an abrupt career-ending blunder for a public affairs officer, instead showed George Shultz in a humane and forgiving mode. It was his first visit to Bonn after becoming secretary of state, and he had cabled strict instructions to his close seventy-eight-year-old friend and mentor, Ambassador Arthur Burns, not to meet him at the airport inasmuch as he was arriving at 2:00 a.m. Other embassy officers were on hand that cold December night to meet him and to perform the usual functions, including distributing press packets to the accompanying traveling journalists.

It was not until the press party had arrived at the hotel that one of the reporters glanced at the press packet and found his lead story right on the cover: it announced in bold letters "Visit of the U.S. Secretary of State Charles P. Shultz." It was a slow news day, and the cover of the press packet found itself displayed on evening network news shows and in newspapers throughout the United States with the comment that the American embassy in Bonn didn't even know the secretary's correct name!

Secretary Shultz treated this gaffe unexpectedly lightly, recalling that it was not the first time this had happened to him. He told us that when he was president of the Bechtel Corporation, his secretary interrupted a board of directors meeting one day with an urgent message that President Carter was phoning him. He took the call and after some friendly chit-chat, President Carter reportedly said, "Well, you know, George, my staff here sometimes doesn't understand me. I wanted to speak with Charles Schultze [an economic adviser to the President], and they connected me with you—so I thought I'd just say hello."

As the thoroughly embarrassed PAO, I made a buck-stops-here attempt to tell Ambassador Burns, a stickler for accuracy, about the blooper perpetrated by his USIS section. He merely smiled and said, "You know, I gave George Shultz and Charles Schultze their first government jobs. Both fine economists."

I reminded the ambassador that most people associated the name Charles Schulz with the cartoonist. He didn't react. I said, "You know, Mr. Ambassador, Peanuts!"

"Never heard of him," came the reply, and that ended the conversation.

More Music

Arthur—we did get on a first-name basis—had no interest in music and failed to understand why it gave me so much pleasure. Now, having digressed intentionally to explain why our time in Bonn had been so fulfilling, I return to my preoccupation—musical performances during our four years in Germany.

Rather than writing about musical experiences chronologically, as I have done up to now, I will cover the subject geographically here. My job required me to travel frequently to USIS branch posts—in Berlin, Hamburg, Düsseldorf, Frankfurt, Stuttgart, and Munich—and to subposts—the German-American Institutes in Kiel, Hannover, Cologne, Heidelberg, Nuremberg, Saarbrücken, and Tübingen. I was thus able to become acquainted with most of the major opera houses and several of the provincial ones in the Federal Republic.

We subscribed to the opera in Bonn, a cross between a major house and a provincial one, and attended some good performances, some mediocre ones, and one really bad one: a production of *Un Ballo in Maschera in which* the action was placed in the bay of Boston in the 1930s on the duke's—here the governor's—pleasure ship. The only mitigating factor was the presence of Carlo Cossutta in the duke's role and Piero Capucilli as Renato.

Compensating for that disaster was an excellent performance of Janáček's *Katya Kabanova*, our first, conducted by Martin Turnovsky and featuring an excellent young soprano, Mechthild Gessendorf, whom we were to hear and enjoy frequently in other productions. We also heard a good performance of Alban Berg's *Lulu* conducted by Jan Krenz. On another occasion we heard a fine performance of *Der Rosenkavalier*, conducted by Martin Turnovsky and featuring Delores Ziegler in the title role, Arlene Saunders as the *Marschallin*, and the aging Karl Riddenbusch as Baron Ochs.

In Bonn we also heard a musically good performance of Bellini's *Norma*, which I love, conducted by Gianfranco Masini and featuring the fiery Mara Zampieri opposite the vocally wonderful Fiorenza Cossotto fighting over the Bulgarian tenor Dimiter Petkov. We also attended a rarely heard *Damnation of Faust* by Hector Berlioz and a *Don Giovanni*, both conducted by Gustav Kuhn. The Mozart was notable primarily for the presence of Renato Bruson as the Don.

We heard the excellent Hildegard Behrens twice in Bonn, once in *Fidelio* with Rene Kollo as Florestan and the other time in *Salome*, conducted by Gustav Kuhn. That performance featured Helga Dernesch as Herodias and Bernd Weikl as John the Baptist. We became acquainted with Behrens because her companion, Seth

Schneidemann, who directed the *Salome,* was the son of a colleague of mine, Harold Schneidemann, who came over from Washington to attend the performance.

I traveled to Berlin regularly, our office there being the most important USIS establishment in the Federal Republic, and was usually able to take in one or more performances at the Deutsche Oper in West Berlin and, occasionally, also the Staatsoper in East Berlin.

I want to mention two outstanding performances of *Don Carlos* at the Deutsche Oper. One, in 1981, was conducted by Francisco Molinari-Pradelli and featured a prime cast of Vasile Moldaveanu in the title role, Mirella Freni as Elisabet, Agnes Baltsa as Eboli, Renato Bruson as Posa, and Nicolai Ghiaurov as the king. In the second, in 1982, the performance was conducted by Stefan Soltesz with an almost equally notable cast: Pilar Lorengar as Elisabet, Stefanie Toczyska as Eboli, Bengt Rundgren as the king, and William Dooley as Posa.

Pilar Lorengar, whose wonderful voice was matched by an unassuming, pleasant, almost placid personality, lived in Berlin with her dentist husband and didn't like to travel. So one was able to hear her often in different roles. Besides her appearance in *Don Carlos,* I had the pleasure of hearing her in *Don Giovanni* (Donna Elvira) and *Otello* (Desdemona).

On one of our rare ventures to East Berlin, Mimi and I attended a production of Mozart's *Idomeneo.* What a disappointment! We had never seen the opera before and anticipated hearing it in the sumptuously rebuilt Staatsoper, the scene of my first opera experiences forty-three years earlier. The production was incomprehensible and the singing mediocre.

Among the many opera houses in Germany, Munich's must be considered one of the best, having the additional advantage of its gorgeous home, rivaled in traditional grandeur perhaps only by Vienna and, now, Dresden. (I have never been in either La Scala or the Paris Opera.) It also has excellent acoustics. In Munich we attended the world premiere of Giuseppe Sinopolis' opera *Lou Salomé* in 1981, conducted by the composer and featuring the fine Karan Armstrong in the title role.

We also heard a topnotch *Simon Boccanegra* in Munich that year, conducted by Miguel Gomez Martinez, with Renato Bruson in the title role, Margaret Price as Amelia, and Robert Lloyd as Fiesco. In 1983 also in Munich, we heard an excellent *Marriage of Figaro,* conducted by Wolfgang Sawallisch, the Munich's music director, and featuring Wolfgang Brendel, Margaret Price, and Edith Mathis among others. Later that year we heard a double bill, conducted by Sawallisch, of Puccini's *Il Tabarro* with Carlo Cossutta, Rosalind Plowright, and Guillermo Sarabia, and *Gianni Schicchi*, featuring Roland Panerei in the title role, Lucia Popp as Lauretta, and Astrid Varnay as Zita.

Our introduction to what is now commonly called "Eurotrash" came about in 1981 in a familiar locale, the Frankfurt Opera, which had been our second home in the early fifties. It was our first hearing of Handel's *Giulio Cesare,* conducted by Ivan Fischer and featuring the excellent American baritone, Michael Devlin, in the title role. (In subsequent productions that we have heard, the title role was usually sung by a contralto.) At the beginning of the second act a golden cage was lowered from the flies in which three nude women cavorted with one another. Their presence and activities as they exhibited themselves throughout the act had, to the best of my understanding, absolutely nothing to do with the action on the stage and remains inexplicable, if provocative, to this day.

Another example of Eurotrash came much later in a production of *Rigoletto* at the equally familiar Deutsche Oper in Berlin. During the brief introduction the curtain rose onto a cellar (presumably in the duke's palace), where the duke was shown raping a nude girl (supposedly Monterone's daughter) on a stone slab that could have been one of the duke's predecessors' sarcophagi.

Other operatic experiences came in the provincial but quite good Krefeld opera house: a production of Borodin's *Prince Igor* in 1983 and, on New Year's Eve 1984, Dominico Cimarosa's *Il Matrimonio Secreto*. At a party later that evening in the home of German friends we became acquainted with another guest, Leonard Slatkin, then the music director of the St. Louis Symphony.

Three other fine opera houses were those in Hamburg, Stuttgart, and Cologne. In Hamburg in 1981 I heard an excellent *Marriage of Figaro*, conducted by Klauspeter Seibel with Hermann Prey as Figaro and Berd Weikl as the count. On another occasion I witnessed a production of *Der Rosenkavalier*, conducted by Silvio Variso, with the three ladies Judith Beckmann, Marjana Lipovsik, and Gabriele Fontana, and the bass, Hans Sotin.

In Stuttgart, I heard a performance of *Tales of Hoffmann* conducted by Kerry Taliaferro, with Janos Korda as Hoffmann and Victor Braun in the three roles of his malevolent pursuer. I also attended a performance of *Cavalleria Rusticana*, conducted by Janos Kulka, with Michail Svetlov as Turrido.

In Cologne, only a twenty-five-minute drive from Bonn, we took in a number of productions, including a *Cenerentola* conducted by Georg Fischer, with Ann Murray in the title role and David Kuebler as her prince; a performance of *Die Meistersinger* conducted by

Hans Wallat, with Theo Adam in the title role; and again, Mimi's favorite, *Un Ballo in Maschera,* conducted by John Pritchard, with Vasile Moldoveanu as the duke and Leo Nucci as Renato.

Switching from opera, I heard many memorable concerts and recitals during our four years in Germany, some together with Mimi and others during my solo travels around the country. I will mention only the truly outstanding ones.

Soon after our arrival in Bonn in July 1980, the American embassy co-hosted the New York Philharmonic under Zubin Mehta. They played the Mahler First Symphony and Strauss's tone poem *Don Quixote,* with the orchestra's principals, Sidney Harth and Lorne Munroe in the solo parts. They were enthusiastically received in Bonn's Beethoven Halle. Next came the Philharmonia Orchestra under Ricardo Muti, playing Beethoven's Seventh Symphony and Third Piano Concerto, with Radu Lupu as soloist.

In 1981, the great Chicago Symphony under Georg Solti came to Bonn, playing Beethoven's Eighth and Bruckner's Fourth Symphonies and giving us a brief opportunity to meet our friend Gyuri again.

Also in Bonn, in 1982, we welcomed the Pittsburgh Symphony under Andre Previn, playing the Haydn Symphony no. 88, the Mahler Symphony no. 10, and the Tchaikovsky Symphony no. 4. Following the Pittsburgh was the National Symphony under Mstislav Rostropovich playing Schumann's Symphony no. 2 and Stravinsky's *Petrushka.* In 1983 Zubin Mehta returned with the Los Angeles Philharmonic, touring under the cosponsorship of the Mattell Toy Company. They played Brahms's Second and Third Symphonies. Mehta came back once more that year, this time with the Israel Philharmonic, playing Mahler's Third Symphony, with the excellent Florence Quivar as soloist.

Among the outstanding recitals we heard in Bonn were those of Pinchas Zuckerman in 1982, Murray Perahia and our close friend, Israela Margalit, in 1983. Israela returned to her piano-playing career after she and Lorin Maazel divorced. It was a double pleasure— personal and artistic—to hear her again, playing Brahms, Chopin, Rachmaninoff, and Kabalevsky.

Israela came to Germany several times while we were there, and we saw each other frequently. In 1981 we heard her playing with the Guerzenich Orchestra, the symphony orchestra of Cologne, under Yuri Abramovich, in Saint Saens's Piano Concerto. In 1982 we went to Frankfurt to hear her play the Schubert Fantasie in C-Major with the Radio Symphony Orchestra under Eliahu Inbol. We traveled to Baden-Baden to hear her in recital. Since our retirement, we have been in touch with her from time to time.

Throughout my travels to other cities in the Federal Republic, I was fortunate to hear a number of excellent concerts and recitals. During 1980 in Berlin, I attended a fine performance of the Brahms *German Requiem* by the Berlin Philharmonic Orchestra under Carl Gorvin, with the soloists Sylvia Geszty and Gerd Feldhoff. In Frankfurt, in 1981, I heard the Museumsorchester, under Rafael Kubelik, play Beethoven's Fifth and Kubelik's own *Symphony in One Movement*. In Düsseldorf, that year we cosponsored a concert of the Utah Symphony Orchestra under Witold Rowicki, playing Mendelsohn's Piano Concerto no. 1, with Karl Engel as soloist, and Mussorgsky's *Pictures at an Exhibition.* It was my second involvement with this regional orchestra, and I was amazed at its excellence.

In Berlin, in 1984, I heard Lorin Maazel conduct the Berlin Philharmonic in a memorable concert, with Claudio Arrau playing the Beethoven Piano Concerto no. 5. This was my last hearing of this remarkable artist. (I remember the first time I heard him—in Kansas City in 1939 or 1940, shortly after my immigration.) Finally, in Munich the same year, I heard the Bavarian Radio Symphony Orchestra, under Guenter Wand, playing Bruckner's Eighth Symphony.

An interruption during my tour in the FRG took me to South Africa on a business trip. Naturally I had to go to a concert of the Capetown Symphony Orchestra, under the young Christian Badea, playing Schumann's Symphony no. 4 and Mozart's Concerto for Flute and Harp.

In 1984 I briefly returned home to Kansas City on a medical emergency involving my mother. While there, I attended a wonderful recital by Emanuel Ax and Yo-Yo Ma playing Schubert, Hindemith, and Kakhmaninou.

In January 1985, our tour in the FRG came to an end. We were invited to a number of friendly farewells, made even more heartfelt because the good-byes marked not only our departure from Bonn but also our retirement from the Foreign Service. Two farewell parties were particularly heartwarming. Ambassador and Mrs. Burns hosted a formal dinner for twenty-four guests. I had formed close professional contacts with all the guests, and Mimi and I had close friendships with some, including Dr. Hildegard Hamm-Bruecher (deputy foreign minister and member of the Bundestag), State Secretary and Mrs. Berndt von Staden, Beate Lindemann (deputy chairman of the Atlantic Bruecke), and in particular the famed Russian writer Lev Kopelev and his wife. The previous year I had assisted the Kopelevs in settling in Cologne after their forced emigration from the Soviet Union.

The other party was a real blast. Hosted by our close friends Bill and Sheila Woessner, it was a dinner dance to which seventy friends had been invited. The affair had an especially appropriate theme, "A Night at the Opera," and guests were invited to come costumed as their favorite opera character (black tie was acceptable for those averse to exposing themselves to ridicule). The dinner menu was distinctive: Scallop Terrine Woglinde, Zwiebel Liebesgetränk, Filet of Beef Falstaff, Insalata Leporello, and Sorbet Mozart. What a send-off!!

Our colleagues and friends in Berlin, not to be outdone, presented me with a unique and touching farewell gift, a monetary contribution to the construction of the new chamber music hall of the Berlin Philharmonic. As evidence of their contribution, I received a numbered red brick in the shape of the chamber music auditorium. To this day, the model sits on a book shelf next to my desk.

Even USIA director Charles Wick sent a congratulatory telegram. We had had a love-hate relationship during his administration, a relationship that ended in friendship. He officiated at my retirement ceremony in Washington on January 31, 1985, where he made one of his typical comments: "In our many discussions over the years I learned that Tom was right 50 percent of the time; and I was wrong 50 percent of the time."[15]

Why retire at age sixty when mandatory retirement was not until age sixty-five? There were several reasons: first, I had worked for the U.S. government the thirty-five years beyond which there could be no further growth in the size of my pension. Second, I was at the top of my Foreign Service career, so there was no incentive to stay longer for promotion. Third, both Mimi's mother and mine were aging and needed our presence, while not in the immediate vicinity, at least within the country. (As it happened, they both lived to ninety-six.) So, another foreign assignment was out of the question, even one as attractive as a chief of mission. And finally, I really did not wish to serve in a policymaking position in Washington in the Reagan administration, as had been suggested, since I largely disagreed with its foreign aims. So the end of our Foreign Service life—a life which had been personally fulfilling—evolved into a new life full of activities as private citizens in Washington.

Act II
Enjoying Retirement in Washington
(1985–Present)

10

Reentering Life in Wasington

I had initially intended to end this tale with my retirement from the Foreign Service; but I found that our subsequent life was so full of cultural activities—opera, concerts, theater and movies—that I decided to record some of these experiences for posterity, here limited to opera.

We moved back into our house in Bethesda which we had rented to a British embassy family, who kept it in tiptop shape. Mimi and I are not gardeners, but we had inherited from our previous owners forty-some rose bushes ringing our garden. These flowers gave us great pleasure during the blooming season but also demanded constant care—spraying against all kinds of diseases and insect invasions, as well as watering and pruning. Gradually over the years the bushes succumbed to various blights and the sunscreen of shade trees, and we finally replaced them with perennial bushes. The only "crops" we harvested yearly were from five cherry tomato plants, which yielded enough tomatoes to satisfy our needs and those of neighbors and friends.

I did some consulting for USIA and several nonprofit organizations, and was asked to join the board of Youth for Understanding (YFU). As one of the two leading teenage youth exchange organizations in this country, YFU brings hundreds of youngsters from various countries to the United States for ten-month home stays, high school attendance, and community involvement. It also sends American teenagers abroad for the same purpose.

While still in Germany, I assisted in starting what became known as the U.S.Congress–German Bundestag Youth Exchange Program. It was an outgrowth of the commemorative year 1983, celebrating three hundred years of German immigration to America.[16]

YFU became one of the principal organizations that operated this unique exchange program. After twenty-five years, the program was still going strong. It has been so successful in terms of the intercultural communication process that I am going to digress, here, from my musical tale, and quote a letter that a German teenager wrote before his return home to Germany after spending a school year in San Jose, California:

> To explore and discover a foreign culture and to live in it may be the most adventuresome and most challenging opportunity there is. Culture itself is rooted in customs, traditions, routine and day-to-day living. To be part of an American family and thus to be wholly integrated into the culture ... presented me with a view of the real United States. The diversity of religions, beliefs and races is universal and exposed me to many different aspects of life. I often got involved with my friends in hot discussions about our countries, but prejudice did not prevail, rather tolerance and bilateral understanding. ... The experience of being an exchange student does not only last a year — it lasts a lifetime. ... In summation, the year in the United States was definitely a high point of my life. I wish every German could have the opportunity to spend a year in the U.S because this is the most effective way to create better understanding between our countries. I will return to Germany with memories of unforgettable experiences, friends and especially my lovely host family, thus taking back a transcontinental, everlasting tie with the United States of America."

In the early nineties, the long term success of this exchange program led the U.S. Congress to enact the Freedom Support Act, which provided for the yearly exchange of about 1,400 youngsters from the former Soviet Union. That program, initiated by Senator Bill Bradley, also continues today as one of the proven public diplomacy initiatives supported by both administration and Congress.

Continuing with my digression from the Washington opera scene, in March 1985 I was invited to give a talk at the University of Pittsburgh on U.S. public diplomacy in Germany. Just before the lecture, I facetiously told my host, Professor Joseph Coffey, that I was tired of talking constantly about political and social tensions between the United States and Germany and would much rather discuss opera in Germany. He blanched, and I hurriedly assured him that I was only joking and went on to speak about U.S.-German communication issues. No sooner had I returned to my hotel after the lecture than I received a call from the head of Pitt's Music Department, asking whether I would agree to give an informal talk on opera in Germany to a group of music students.

The event took place that afternoon in a small auditorium crowded with students. In the middle of the fourth or fifth row among the informally clad young men and women sat a lovely lady in a white dress, wearing a large red hat. During my entire talk I kept wondering who that incongruously dressed woman might be, so attentively listening to what I was saying.

At the end of the lecture and discussion, she came up to me and introduced herself: "My name is Millie Posvar, and my husband is president of the university. I was interested in your talk because I got my start singing opera in Stuttgart in the late forties."

I laughed. "You must be Mildred Miller, or rather 'Mildred Müller,' and I heard you singing the third lady—the mezzo— in *Die Zauberflöte* in Stuttgart in 1949." She looked at me unbelieving, and I added, "In the early 1950s I heard you in Met Saturday afternoon broadcasts when you sang Cherubino in practically every *Marriage of Figaro* performance, usually with John Brownlee as the Count." That earned me an immediate dinner invitation. Joined by her husband and my hosts, we then proceeded to the Pittsburgh Opera Theater, which Millie Posvar directed. The company performed Menotti's *The Telephone* and Hindemith's seven-minute opera *Hin and Zurück* (*There and Back*). A delightful evening!

In March 1985, USIA asked me to evaluate the effectiveness of the Salzburg Seminar. Founded shortly after World War II and located in Leopoldskron, a lovely and historic eighteenth century palace on the outskirts of Salzburg, the seminar was financed largely by the Austrian and U.S. governments for the purpose of bringing together young professionals from various nations for intensive examination of vital issues—political, technological, social, economic, scientific, and cultural. In 1985 the USIA administration was looking at the Salzburg Seminar with a critical eye, questioning its annual operating grant.

After spending a week observing a seven-day conference on public health issues, I came away highly impressed with the Seminar, in part because it provided a unique platform for Palestinian and Israeli public health specialialists and Indian and Pakistani doctors, along with participants from the United States and several other countries, to spend a week living and talking together about common issues and problems. My report, later cited in the *Congressional Record,* helped continue USIA's support for the organization.

Incidental to this trip to Salzburg was a fortuitous two-day visit to Vienna, where I attended a performance of Tchaikovsky's *Pique Dame,* conducted by Dimitri Kitaenko at the Vienna Staatsoper. It featured the excellent Natalia Troitskaya and the by-now legendary Christa Ludwig in the seminal role of the Old Countess.

In the fall of 1985 David Newsom, then the Associate Dean of the School of Foreign Service at Georgetown University, invited me to join with him in teaching a course in Intercultural Communication. That seminar evolved the following year into a new course in the Practice of Public Diplomacy, which I then taught by myself for the next three years. (It was only the second public diplomacy course taught at a university, the other being at the Fletcher School of Law and Diplomacy at Tufts University, where I had taught it during 1975–76.) At Newsom's urging, I authored *Communicating with the World: U.S. Public Diplomacy Overseas* (St. Martin's Press, 1990) while at Georgetown. At the time it was the only textbook on the subject. Though now out-of-print, it is still used at Georgetown and other universities, with students apparently able to obtain the book through the Internet.

Now to the music! Rather than recording our attendance at opera events chronologically, I will report on performances at individual institutions, and then only the outstanding opera productions, as there are so many—altogether some 365 opera and 160 concert and recital performances between 1985 and 2006.

11

The Washington National Opera

The Washington National Opera (WNO) had evolved since the 1970s into an ever-expanding artistic enterprise. It featured some excellent singing, like the 1985 *Don Giovanni* conducted by John Mauceri and including Renato Bruson in the title role, Philip Langridge as Don Ottavio, and the ladies Karen Huffstad, the wonderful, emerging Karita Mattila, and Faith Esham.

Rarities in 1986 included Rimsky-Korsakov's *The Tsar's Bride*, conducted by Mstislav Rostropovich in top form, and Menotti's *Goya*, conducted by Rafael Frühbeck de Burgos and featuring Placido Domingo in a title role not worthy, in my view, of his artistry.

In 1987 the novelty was Mascagni's *L'Amico Fritz*, while in 1988 the outstanding production was Massenet's *Cendrillon*, conducted by Mario Bernardi and featuring the incomparable Frederica von Stade (repeating her success from 1979), Tracy Dahl, Suzanne Mentzer, Joyce Castle, and Alan Held.

The year 1989 brought Stephen Paulus's *The Postman Always Rings Twice*, Tchaikovsky's *Pique Dame*, and an exemplary *Cosi fan tutte*, conducted by Leon Fleischer, who at that time was not playing the piano because of a debilitating ailment in his right hand.

In 1990, we heard Dominick Argento's *Aspern Papers*, conducted by Philip Brunelle, and featuring a young and stellar cast that included Pamela South, Susan Graham, Katherine Cezinsky, and David Kuebler. That year we also saw Maria Ewing's rendition of the "Dance of the Seven Veils" in Richard Strauss's *Salome*, which ended in the soprano's complete unveiling. She was okay vocally too! Massenet's *Werther* was also on the program that year.

With one exception, 1991 was the only disastrous season we experienced at the Washington Opera. The exception was a good production of Menotti's *The Saint of Bleeker Street*, conducted by Steven Mercurio. Purcell's *King Arthur*, a lovely Baroque opera, was not stylistically right for the Washington Opera, although it was conducted by the capable Stephen Lord and featured the fine voices of Amy Burton, Elizabeth Comeaux, Kurt Ollmann and Ingvar Halvorsen. The adjective "disastrous" applied to both *Don Carlos* and *Don Giovanni*, which were performed by a two-piano team that replaced the striking orchestra. It would have been better to cancel the two productions.

The novelties of the 1992 season were the Chinese opera *Savage Land* and Handel's *Agrippina*, again conducted by Stephen Lord but this time stylistically in tune with the Baroque period.

The 1993 season boasted several outstanding performances, starting with the delightful production of Janáček's *Cunning Little Vixen*, conducted by Christopher Keene, and featuring the charming and talented Mary Mills in the title role. A production of Donizetti's *Anna Bolena*, conducted by Edoardo Müller, featured Nelli Miricioiu in the title role. In earlier roles, such as Manon, Miricioiu had displayed a lovely voice and dramatic characterization, which had made her a favorite here; in this production, however, she appeared beyond her prime, and her voice suggested the unreliability that had apparently hampered her international career.

In 1994 the premiere of Dominick Argento's *The Dream of Valentine* passed rather unremarkably. The season featured two operas, Strauss's *Ariadne auf Naxos* and Mozart's *Marriage of Figaro*, conducted by Heinz Fricke, who had assumed the musical directorship of the Washington Opera two years earlier. Although late in his career—he had been musical director of the Staatsoper in Berlin for many years—Fricke made a significant contribution in developing the Washington Opera's orchestra into one of the major opera ensembles in the country.

Three rarely performed operas highlighted the 1995 season: Handel's *Semele*, conducted by Martin Perlman and featuring tenor Richard Croft, countertenor David Daniels, and sopranos Patricia Spence and Brenda Harris; Eugene d'Albert's *Tiefland*, conducted by Heinz Fricke; and Samuel Barber's *Vanessa*, conducted by Andre Manson and featuring Charlotte Hellekant and Elizabeth Holleque. That year also brought Verdi's *Luisa Miller*; Bizet's *Carmen*, with Dennyce Graves (Wolf Trap alumna) in the title role, and Mary Mills as Micaela; and an outstanding *Rosenkavalier*, conducted by Fricke, with Helen Donath as the Marschallin.

In 1996, the WNO introduced another new work, Hans Krasna's *Verlobung im Traum* (*Engagement in a Dream*), and brought Boito's *Mephistofele*, conducted by John de Main, starring Samuel Ramey in the title role, and featuring tenor William Joiner and a deteriorating Nell Miriciou (her last appearance here).

A new era at the Washington National Opera began in 1997 with the appointment of Placido Domingo as artistic director. Besides possessing one of the world's great tenor voices, he has been a fine musician and a consummate artist throughout the years and still to this day, at 67 years of age.

Highly positive factors of his appointment were his ability to attract funding and his artistic vision, which together enabled the company to expand into a prominent training ground for young artists. On the negative side, in my view, Domingo spreads himself too thin—directing the Los Angeles Opera, running "Operalia," singing in the major opera houses of the world (frequently in new roles), conducting opera here and abroad, all on top of directing one of the nation's principal opera houses. Indeed, when does he sleep?!

As a result the WNO does not consistently live up to the high standard one should expect from a house that asks top prices— nearly equal to those of the Met and Chicago operas. Though the orchestra under Heinz Fricke is tops, the productions sometimes seem too visually extravagant and lacking in substance and rationale (fortunately not approaching, however, the "Eurotrash" one frequently finds abroad these days). The voices, while often outstanding, occasionally fail to live up to expectations.

Furthermore, Domingo himself has disappointed some of his loyal fans in the past couple of years by not giving as much of himself as in the past, when he sang one major role every season—Parsifal, Le Cid, Herman (in *Queen of Spades*), Siegmund, and Idomeneo. Recently, in Washington, he has limited himself to roles in Zarzuela or to snippets from an operatic potpourri—whereas in other opera houses he continues to sing major roles. These quibbles should not, however, detract from his major contribution in making the WNO a leading musical institution in this country.

Unfortunately, in 1997, his first season as artistic director Domingo picked a role that was unworthy of his talents—the lead in *Il Guarany*, by the nineteenth century Brazilian composer Carlos Gomez. He sang dressed in a ridiculous native Indian costume that generated a number of humorous comments. His leading lady was Veronica Villaroel, his frequent partner in subsequent performances.

Two other productions in 1997 should be mentioned because they are rarely performed: Douglas Moore's *Baby Doe*, conducted by Keith Lockhart, featuring Elizabeth Comeaux in the title role and Richard Stillwell as her husband; and Mozart's *La Finta Giardiniera*, conducted by Patrick Summers.

The 1998 season included Puccini's *La Rondine,* conducted by Emmanuel Villaume, featuring the delightful Ainhoa Arteta; Gounod's *Romeo and Juliet,* conducted by Bertrand de Billy, with the emerging star Elizabeth Futral and Marcello Giordani; and a *Don Giovanni* conducted by Fricke in which the Croft brothers—Dwayne in the title role and Richard as Don Ottavio—performed with distinction.

The 1999 season brought several productions that stand out in memory. One was Umberto Giordano's *Fedora,* conducted by Roberto Abbado and starring the aging but still wonderful Mirella Freni and her contemporary and equally wonderful Placido Domingo. Next came Delibes's *Samson et Dalila,* which Domingo conducted—the first time we saw him in the orchestra pit rather than on stage. Careerwise, this may have been a smart move for him, and, in my view, he performed adequately if still somewhat tentatively. The Samson was the much anticipated—but prematurely so—Jose Cura, while Denyce Graves's Dalila more than met expectations. She was the temptress incarnate, both dramatically and vocally.

Samuel Ramey sang *Boris Godunov* that year, and Heinz Fricke conducted *Tristan und Isolde,* a rare production of a Wagner opera at the WNO. We last heard it in this house in 1980.

The following year, 2000, introduced a real find, a wonderful young soprano, Anna Netrebko, in *Rigoletto,* conducted by Fricke. Since then, she has become one of the genuine stars of international opera, but we heard her here first.

A novelty that year was Massenet's *Le Cid,* the opera Placido Domingo chose for his star appearance that season. Carlisle Floyd's *Susannah* received its first WNO production, as did two other relative rarities: Donizetti's *I Puritani* and Handel's *Julio Caesar.* Will Crutchfield conducted *Julio Caesar,* which featured an outstanding cast with Viveca Genaux in the title role, and Catherine Keen, Marguerite Krull, and Hei-Kyung Hong.

In the 2000–2001 season, *Parsifal* was Domingo's choice for his annual appearance, which Heinz Fricke conducted in a marvelous performance that included the exemplary singing of Matti Salminen and Alan Held. Domingo also conducted a forgettable production of *Il Trovatore,* while a *Marriage of Figaro* conducted by Fricke stands out in memory for Anna Netrebko's second appearance at the WNO.

Fricke also conducted a production of Puccini's *Turandot,* one of my least favorite operas. I mention it here because of Alexandra Marc's fine singing in the title role, despite a physical handicap that, I understand, keeps her off many opera stages.

In the 2001–2002 season, Heinz Fricke's conducting of *Cosi fan tutte* stood out, in part because of the fine ensemble work by the brothers Croft—Richard and Dwayne—and their "lovers," Ainhoa Arteto and Joyce di Donato, and the "co-conspirators" Simone Alberghini and Marguerite Krull.

Domingo's singing contribution that season was in the role of Herman in Tchaikovsky's *Queen of Spades*. The ever-fascinating Elena Obraztsova was the countess, Galina Gorchakova sang the role of Lisa, and Heinz Fricke did his usual excellent job of conducting the performance.

The start of a major renovation of the Opera House bifurcated the 2002–2003 season of the WNO. The first part of the season took place in the Opera House and distinguished itself by several remarkable performances. One was a production of Samuel Barber's *Vanessa*, conducted by Emmanuel Joel, made memorable by the last opera appearance of Dame Kiri te Kanawa in the title role. She was truly breathtaking in her vocal dramatization.

In addition, Claire Gibaul (new to me and excellent) conducted a fine performance of *Idomeneo*, with Domingo in the title role, and an outstanding Ana Netrebko as Ilia. I must also note the artistry of Elizabeth Futral in a performance of *Lucia di Lammermoor*.

The second part of the season took place in Constitution Hall, which had been reconfigured to accommodate opera productions. In spite of my misgivings and some formidable difficulties, the WNO carried it off with considerable success. Whatever objections I entertained to some productions were not caused by the deficiencies of the hall. Heinz Fricke conducted an outstanding production of *Die Walküre*, with Domingo singing Siegmund beautifully and a wonderful new Sieglinde, Anja Kampe. Linda Watson as Bruenhilde, Alan Held as Wotan, and a young and attractive troop of Walkyries completed this satisfying production.

Fricke also conducted a production of *Aida* that featured the almost over-the-top singing of the remarkable Maria Guleghina. The production adapted to the stage deficiencies of Constitution Hall by creating dramatic visual images by way of video projections.

Back in the renovated Opera House in 2004, Richard Hickox conducted a fine production of Benjamin Britten's *Billy Budd,* with excellent characterizations by Dwayne Croft, Robin Leggate, and, the by now a bit wobbly Samuel Ramey. Domingo's involvement in that year's repertory was limited to Frederico Torroba's Zarzuela, *Luisa Fernanda*.

The season's novelty was an excellent production of Andre Previn's *A Streetcar Named Desire*, which to my mind, did justice to the drama inherent in the story.

In 2005 Domingo conducted an incomprehensible production of Verdi's equally incomprehensible yet superbly melodic *I Vespri Siciliani*, with top-notch singing by Maria Guleghina, Franco Farina, Vitalij Kowaljow, and Lado Ataneli.

That year also saw the world premiere of Scott Wheeler's *Democracy* (performed in the Lissner Auditorium), conducted by Anne Mason with some excellent singing by Robert Baker, William Parcher, Amanda Squitieri, Keri Alkema, Lee Poulis, and Matthew Wolf. On first hearing this imaginatively produced opera, Mimi and I liked it very much, especially in its approachability and ability to engage the listener.

WNO's 50th anniversary gala consisted of scenes from three different operas—Act II of Giordano's *Fedora*, Act IV of Verdi's *Otello*, and Act III of Lehar's *Merry Widow*. For me they were unsatisfactory snippets that made no dramatic or musical sense other than to display "our" tenor's remarkably fine voice. The internationally recognized sopranos Sylvie Valayre (in *Fedora*) and Barbara Fritoli (in *Otello*) matched Domingo note for note.

We also heard a repeat of a previous production of *Samson and Dalila*, this time conducted by Domingo, with the excellent Olga Borodina, Carl Tanner, and Alan Held in the leading roles. And one other memorable production was Gershwin's *Porgy and Bess*, conducted by Wayne Marshall. Exceptionally well done, it featured Kevin Short and Morenike Fadayomi in the title roles, Alyson Cambridge as Clara, Lester Green as Crown, Dara Rahming, and Lester Lynch.

In 2006 we heard *Das Rheingold* as the initial segment of the first *Ring* to be produced by the WNO. Conducted with his usual excellence by Heinz Fricke and directed imaginatively by Francesca Zambella, the opera featured Robert Hale as Wotan, the superb Gordon Hawkins as Alberich, Elizabeth Bishop as Fricka, John Marcus Bindel and Jeffrey Wells as the giants Fasolt and Fafner, and Elena Zaremba as Erda—all very good.

There was a delightful, excruciatingly funny production of Rossini's *L'Italiana in Algeri*, conducted by Riccardo Frizza, with Olga Borodina in the title role, and Lyubov Petrova, Juan Diego Flores, and Ildar Abrazakov in the other leading parts.

The last opera of the WNO's 2006 season—and the last one to be mentioned in this chapter—was a production of Mozart's *La Clemenza di Tito* conducted by Fricke. Musically superb, it included as fine a Sesto as I have heard in Marina Domashenko and an excellent ensemble, consisting of Tatiana Pavloskaya, Jossie Perez, and Michael Schade.

12

The Washington Concert Opera

If one were to ask for originality and consistency in musical values, there is nothing finer in this city than the Washington Concert Opera (WCO). We were enticed by the WCO in 1988, its second season of existence, when we read that it was going to perform two operas that were relatively seldom produced — Massenet's *Werther* and Bellini's *I Capuletti ed I Montecchi* (the Romeo and Juliet story).

The WCO iconoclastically presents its productions at George Washington University's Lisner Auditorium without scenery, costumes, or stage action. The orchestra, chorus, and conductor occupy almost the entire stage (which is limited in space, preventing presentations of most Strauss, Berlioz, and Wagner operas). The singing actors come out on stage only when they have something to sing or say. Conductor, orchestra, and singers convey the opera's story solely through their articulation of the music and text.

All performances of the WCO employ surtitles — a *sine qua non*, I am convinced, for the comprehension and enjoyment of all operas, whether staged or, as here, in concert form. This is true whether in a foreign language or in English since texts, especially sung by female voices and ensembles, are usually incomprehensible. (This comment will be ridiculed by purists who probably know all foreign and English language librettos from memory.)

To do opera in concert form well requires artists of the highest caliber. Stephen Crout, the founder and musical director of the WCO until 2001, is such an artist. Not only is he a gifted musician and fine conductor, but he also has a knack for picking the right singers for the right part and creating an integrated ensemble. He is also an excellent teacher, as demonstrated in his master classes; he has an uncanny ability to address simultaneously the participating students and the auditing audience.

I am recording chronologically all WCO performances for two reasons other than our enjoyment of them: one, because the repertory of the WCO included a number of relatively infrequently performed works, and two, because most of the artists—exceptions will be noted—were outstanding in their roles even though some of them were relatively early in their careers. All operas were selected, produced and conducted by Stephen Crout.

The first two productions we attended in 1988 immediately hooked us for the future. Massenet's *Werther* featured Jerry Hadley (at his best at the time), Diana Montague, and bass Alan Held, a recent Wolf Trap alumnus.[17] Bellini's *I Capuletti ed Montecchi* featured Mimi Lerner and a young Hei-Kyung Hong in an excellent duo performance.

In 1989 the WCO produced *Ariadne auf Naxos*, the only Strauss opera written for a small enough orchestra to fit onto the Lisner stage. It featured an outstanding cast: Alexandra Marc (on our first hearing) as Ariadne, Catherine Ciesinski as the composer, Tracy Dahl as Zerbinetta, Frederick West, and Alan Held. The second production that year was *Lakme* by Delibes, with Tracy Dahl in the title role.

In 1990 it was Bellini's *I Puritani*, with the delightful Sumi Jo and, unfortunately, Chris Merritt, who must be my *bête noir* in the tenor category. He appears on the world's concert stages, but I don't understand why. He yells, scoops, flounders on and off pitch, and on that day convinced me to avoid performances in which he appears. The production also featured the always dependable Jeffrey Wells and the young Charles Workman.

The second opera of the 1990 season was Donizetti's *Lucretia Borgia* with Nelli Miricioiu in fine voice. In 1991 there was only one opera, Donizetti's *La Favorita*, with two outstanding singing artists, Florence Quivar, and Elizabeth Futral, fresh from Wolf Trap.

In 1992 Deborah Voigt—we heard her first here—brought forth cheers, singing the role of Agathe in Carl Maria von Weber's *Der Freischütz*, while Donizetti's *Anna Bolena* elicited similar audience reactions for the three female artists, Nellie Miriciou, Denyce Graves, and Judith Forst, with tenor Paul Groves holding his own.

Renee Fleming singing Dvořák's *Russalka* was a sensational highlight of the 1993 season. There are few musical moments that affect me like her singing of "O Silver Moon" from that opera. Verdi's *I Vespri Siciliani* in the same year was a disappointment because of the damage done to the melodious opera by Chris Merritt on his second and final appearance with the WCO. I asked Stephen Crout why he had engaged Merritt again after the experience with *I Puritani*, and he replied, "You know, I asked myself the same question while conducting the second act." For the record, Carol Vaness, a bit so-so, sang the role of Elena in that opera.

In the 1994 performance of Bellini's *Norma*, Nelly Miriciou and Sonia Ganassi sang beautifully, but Gegam Gregorian appeared to be sight-reading throughout the evening, requiring frequent cuing from the conductor. That season, a redeeming Ben Heppner was a fine tenor as Chenier in Giordano's *Andrea Chenier*.

In 1995 Gounod's *Romeo and Juliet* featured the delightful Hei-Kyung Hong as Juliet, the no-longer-so youthful Richard Leach as Romeo, and the three emerging Wolf Trap alumni, Margaret Lattimore, Eric Owens, and Jeff Mattsey. The one and only Wagner experience came that year by way of *Der Fliegende Holländer*, with a marvelous James Morris in the title role and Frances Ginzer as Senta.

In 1996, Denyce Graves's fabulous voice and stage allure created a memorable temptress in Delibes's *Samson et Dalila*; and Verdi's *Ernani* sparkled primarily in the secondary roles sung by Gordon Hawkins, Mark Doss, and the newcomer Theodore Green, a fine young tenor.

Another early Verdi opera, *Attila*, was performed in 1997. That same year Bellini's *La Sonnambula* introduced a young silver-voiced soprano, the sparkling Maureen O'Flynn, ably supported by Lynette Tapia, Paul Austin Kelly, and Jeffrey Wells.

Another outstanding soprano, Patricia Racette, graced Rossini's *Guillaume Tell* in 1998; and Ambrose Thomas's seldom performed *Hamlet* completed the 1998 season, featuring the artists Annick Massis, Russell Braun, and Elizabeth Bishop.

Maureen O'Flynn returned in 1999 to sing in Donizetti's *Linda di Chamonix* with the excellent mezzo-soprano Theodora Hanslowe, who later that year joined with Sumi Jo to perform in Bellini's *I Capuletti ed Montecchi*—the second time the WCO performed this opera.

Bizet's *Les Pecheurs de Perles* (*The Pearl Fishers*) opened the WCO's 2000 season. It featured a young tenor, Gregory Turay, another Wolf Trap alumnus who has gone on to a fine operatic career. He was joined by two other first-rate artists, Ned Barth and Jennifer Welsh. A second memorable WCO performance that year was Janáček's *Jenufa*, with two marvelous artists, Patricia Racette and Eva Urbanova.

The 2001 season brought Bellini's *Il Pirata*, with a now seriously deteriorating Nelli Miriciou on the WCO stage for the last time. It is sad that any number of fine artists, whose voices one wants to remember from the apex of their careers, don't seem to know when to quit, so that one is left with only vocal remains.

Unfortunately, it was also Stephen Crout's last production. He had decided to depart from Washington, leaving behind a truly impressive legacy of outstanding musical performances. Without Crout's leadership, the WCO went through a year of crisis until it engaged a new musical director, Antony Walker, who took charge of the company in 2003. I am happy to note that he has maintained the high musical standards of his predecessor. Walker's first two productions in 2003 were Berlioz's *Beatrice and Benedict* and Verdi's early *Stiffelio*, both well executed and well received.

In 2004, Walker chose two seldom heard operas, Donizetti's *Roberto Devereux,* and Rossini's *La Donna del Lago.* In the Rossini, he presented the outstanding young lyric tenor, Lawrence Brownlee, another Wolf Trap alumnus on his way to great things.

In 2005, the WCO presented Verdi's *Luisa Miller* and the double bill of Puccini *Il Tabarro* and Mascagni's *Cavalleria Rusticana*; and in April 2006 Antony Walker conducted the rarely performed Rossini opera *Tancredi.* One reason this opera has never been done professionally in this country, despite its tuneful score, is that the story makes no sense whatsoever: the libretto suggests three different endings. The second reason is the many, excrutiatingly difficult coloratura arias that both the female and male artists have to tackle. The cast was exemplary: Sarah Coburn, Stephanie Blythe, and Lawrence Brownlee—all Wolf Trap alumni—were literally breathtaking (no pun intended) with their long vocal lines and fantastic embellishments, beautifully executed. A total singing experience.

A Washington Concert Opera production of Bellini's *I Puritani* that we heard in September 2007 featured two of the Tancredi performers, Sara Coburn and Larry Brownlee. The following excerpt is part of the *Washington Post* September 25 review of the opera:

> For a few magical hours...soprano Sarah Coburn and tenor Lawrence Brownlee seemed to be the world's best opera singers....[T]heir sweet and radiant voices climbed to stratospheric heights and sped effortlessly through hairpin turns....Undoubtedly, the evening featuring these young singers will rank as a high point in the WCO's adventuresome 20-year history....Coburn's coloratura technique was flawless, each note hit squarely, never ruffling Bellini's following line. Brownlee's Arturo was simply a joy to hear. His voice is supple, strong and seamlessly produced throughout the register. It would be impossible to improve the performance....The entire team was cast from strength, with exceptional performances from David Pittsinger whose chocolate-smooth bass-baritone melded beautifully...with

baritone Stephen Powell....Artistic director Antony Walker enticed vigor and subtlety from the orchestra and chorus, again proving that the WCO is one of Washington's most vital musical institutions.

Mr. Walker is to be congratulated on maintaining the fine reputation of the WCO by continuing to present interesting operas with outstanding casts. The future looks good.

13

Teaching in Kansas City and Vienna

In 1990 my aging mother in Kansas City needed increased personal attention from me, her only child. At the same time, the University of Missouri–Kansas City (UMKC), which had awarded me an honorary Doctor of Laws degree in 1986, invited me to teach as an adjunct professor in the College of Arts and Sciences. I began teaching at UMKC in the fall of 1990, alternating semesters with "Intercultural Communications" and "The Practice of Public Diplomacy."

I learned quickly that I had to adjust my teaching considerably, taking into account the difference between Georgetown and UMKC students' qualifications and academic background and university requirements. Furthermore, the two institutions differed in available research resources. As there were no language requirements for a BA degree at UMKC, for instance, I could not demand that students read foreign newspapers or periodicals. Since there were fewer foreign publications available at UMKC than at Georgetown or at the many foreign embassies in Washington, I could not make familiarity with foreign publications a requirement in either of my two courses. Finally, because no foreign students participated in my courses at UMKC, in contrast to Georgetown, where at least one-third of the students were foreign-born, I could not pose the differences in cultures and societies as a stimulating ingredient in student interaction. The one thing students at both schools had in common, however, was their enthusiasm for participating in these courses and their interest in the subject matter.

My arrangements with the university required that I be present for two weeks at the beginning of the semester, when I would conduct twelve hours of intensive seminar work. During the following six weeks the students would conduct their research and draft their papers. I would then return to Kansas City for another two weeks for further intensive seminar work. This arrangement enabled me to spend two weeks every other month with my mother, thus satisfying my filial obligations.

Since the discipline of public diplomacy is a relatively new area of study, I quote from the syllabus to give the reader an understanding of the importance of public diplomacy both as an academic discipline and as a profession, as well as why I have devoted thirty-five years of my life to the subject:

> In an ever-shrinking world of interdependent nations, international relations have exceeded the confines of traditional diplomacy, in which foreign ministries conduct the affairs and keep the peace among national states. Exploding communications technologies, conflicting ideologies, rising nationalism, and interactive economic, environmental, health, and population problems have forced governments to communicate directly with foreign publics in an effort to achieve broad understanding for their nations' ideas and ideals, their institutions and culture, their national goals and current policies. This governmental process of communicating with foreign publics rather than only with foreign governments is known as *public diplomacy*. It has become an integral part of the conduct of a nation's foreign affairs, and it has therefore become both an academic and a professional discipline.[18]

Naturally, while in Kansas City I partook of the Kansas City Lyric Opera's offerings. I was aided and abetted by my childhood friend, Ed Kander, development director of the Lyric Opera and older brother of the composer John Kander, mentioned earlier. I became friends with Evan Luskin, the Lyric Opera's managing director, and also acquainted with Russell Patterson, the opera's long-time artistic director. I was occasionally quite critical of Patterson's conducting, even though I recognized his devotion to the Lyric Opera and his success in making it a creditable institution.

Ann Kander, Ed's wife and an active supporter of the Lyric Opera, persuaded me to give an introductory lecture at UMKC for a new production of *Der Rosenkavalier* in September 1987. Entitled "Rosenkavaliers I Have Known," it gave me a chance to wallow verbally in some of the wonderful performances I have witnessed, starting with the never-to-be forgotten production in Berlin in 1950, conducted by Erich Kleiber, with the legendary Tiana Lemnitz.

I attended some fifteen performances of the K.C. Lyric Opera, mostly of the standard repertory. I will mention here only two seldom performed works, Mark Blitzstein's *Regina,* in an excellently sung and acted production, and Menotti's *Saint of Bleeker Street*, equally well done.

In the summer of 1991 I was invited by a consortium of the Austrian Diplomatic Academy, Georgetown University, and USIA to conduct a three-week seminar in Vienna on public diplomacy for young diplomats from Poland, Hungary, and Czechoslovakia. It was a successful experiment. The seventeen participants, almost all graduates from the former Soviet Institute of International Relations (IMEMO) in Moscow, took to the idea of communicating with foreign publics—an idea new to them—as an important element of their diplomatic careers. They participated enthusiastically in the give and take of the course which took place on the premises of the ornate eighteenth-century Austrian Diplomatic Academy.

The one disappointment of my three-week stay in Vienna with Mimi was the absence of live opera or, for that matter, any live music, because all opera and concert activities had moved to Salzburg for the festival there. However, since 1991 happened to be the 200th anniversary of Mozart's death, the city fathers had organized nightly filmed performances of Mozart's operas on the plaza in front of Vienna's Rathaus (city hall). One opera that we had never heard before was *Mitridate*, a dated film production but interesting for its novelty. Frequent museum visits and a weekend trip to Graz—no music there either—provided the cultural content of the trip.

My mother passed away in November 1994 at the age of 96. I found the frequent commuting, now solely for my UMKC teaching, burdensome. The spring semester in 1995 thus became my last one in academia.

14

A Plethora of Other Opera Experiences

Back home in Washington we enjoyed other opera performances not yet mentioned in this narrative. In addition to the Washington National Opera, the Washington Concert Opera (and the Wolf Trap Opera Company detailed in the next chapter), we had also subscribed to the Summer Opera at Catholic University since 1986. We were initially drawn to this professional opera company by an excellent performance of Janáček's *Katya Kabanova*, followed over the next twenty years by some forty opera performances. I shall mention here only those of particular interest: Donizetti's *Maria Stuarda* ('89), *Roberto Devereux* ('90), and *Anna Bolena* ('91); Poulenc's *Dialogue of the Carmelites* ('94), Bertolt Brecht's *Three Penny Opera* ('96), Erich Korngold's *Die Tote Stadt* ('98), Janáček's *Jenufa* ('01), Richard Strauss's *Ariadne auf Naxos* ('02), and Puccini's *Suor Angelica* ('02).

The Summer Opera company must have been especially gratified by Tim Page's review in the *Washington Post* of its 2006 *I1 Trovatore* production, with which I heartily agree. He wrote, "The Summer Opera Theater Company's production of Verdi's *I1 Trovatore*...is startlingly good—far better, on almost every level, than stagings I've seen at the Kennedy Center and even New York's Metropolitan Opera."

We attended a number of performances of the Opera Theater of Northern Virginia, primarily because it presented works that were rarely if ever performed elsewhere; to wit, Bizet's *Doctor Miracle*, Milhaud's *Poor Sailor*, Rossini's *Love on Trial*, Puccini's *Le Villi*, Lee Hoiby's *Scarf*, and Daniel Auber's *Fra Diavolo*. They did not feature the finest of voices or production values, but for the most part they were professionally and enthusiastically presented and were valuable in filling gaps in the opera canon.

Occasionally we traveled to Baltimore when the Baltimore Opera presented morsels not to be missed. In 1987 we heard an excellent performance of *Norma*, conducted by Anton Guadagno and featuring Johanna Meier in the title role, Ashley Putnam as Adalgisa, and the aging Jerome Hines as Oroveso. In 1993, we heard a good *Nabucco*, conducted by Joseph Rescigno, who did a novel thing. During intermission, he appeared in the foyer and asked for the audience's attention. He told them to open their programs to the page with the notes and text of the famed Prisoners' Chorus, and to follow his baton as he rehearsed them in "Va pensiero." Then, in Act III, as the prisoners entered the hall from the rear and marched down to the stage, singing "Va pensiero," he turned around and conducted the audience in the last stanza. Thus we can claim to having "sung" in a performance of *Nabucco*.

I prefer not to comment on a Baltimore Opera performance of *Fidelio* we attended. But, I gladly praise a performance of Shostakovich's *Lady Macbeth of Mtsensk* in 2003, conducted by Christian Badea, with Karen Huffstadt in the title role. I had heard this shattering work earlier at the Frankfurt Opera in 1995 while on a lecture tour in Germany. Guido Johannes Rumstadt conducted, with the American soprano Kristine Ciesinsky in the title role. More recently, I met Mr. Rumstadt, when he had just conducted Telemann's *Orpheus* at the Wolf Trap Opera Company. I asked whether it was his father I had heard conduct *Lady Macbeth of Mtsensk* in Frankfurt in the early 1990s, and he laughed, saying it was he who had been the conductor.

One other fine performance we heard in Baltimore was Bellini's *I Puritani* in 2004, conducted by Steven White, with Elizabeth Futral performing beautifully as usual, well supported by Gregory Kunde, and Mikhail Svetlov. We limited our attendance at the Baltimore Opera House because, though the hall has good acoustics, it is uncomfortable to sit in, with insufficient knee room even for a short person like myself, narrow aisles, and limited bathroom facilities that cause long and anxious waiting lines during intermission.

Going back to 1991, we were in Seattle visiting close friends, Sylvia and Gerry Goldstein, who had persuaded us to come in part by dangling in front of us a rare performance of Prokofiev's *War and Peace*, an opera we had wanted to hear for a long time. (While we were in Moscow in the late 1950s, Prokofiev's operas were not in favor with the regime.) It was a terrific production, with Moscow nearly going up in flames in front of the audience during the last act. Conducted by Mark Ermler, it featured, among many other fine voices, Vladimir Chernov and Sheri Greenwald. It was well worth the trip!

Other memorable performances in the 1990s included Mozart's *La Clemenza di Tito*, heard in Dresden in 1995. While on a lecture tour in Germany, I had made the almost obligatory sidetrip to the Saxony capital to visit the gorgeously reconstructed, rococo Semper Oper and to hear *La Clemenza* in a handsome production, led by Hans Zimmer, that featured excellent singing by Hans Peter Blockwitz, Claudia Kunz, and Lani Poulson, the latter two new to me.

Back in Washington we attended a number of productions by the Virginia Opera, which performed regularly at the George Mason University in nearby Fairfax, Virginia. In 1998 we heard, for the first time, Copland's *Tender Land*, which featured Washington's own excellent mezzo-soprano, Elizabeth Bishop. In 1999 we heard Gluck's *Orfeo et Euridice* with Gwendolyn Jones, Sujung Kim, and Nancy Curtis. I should note that all the Virginia Opera productions we heard (save one, not mentioned here) were conducted by its able music director Peter Mark.

In the spring of 2000 we joined other members of the Washington Concert Opera Guild on a tour to Houston to hear the world premiere of Carlisle Floyd's opera *Cold Sassy Tree*. On first hearing, it was a delightful composition expertly presented. The Houston Opera, famous for premiering new works, did an outstanding job. The conductor was Patrick Summers, artistic director of the company, and the cast included Patricia Racette, Dean Peterson, Margaret Lloyd, John McVeigh, and Christopher Schaldenbrand.

A bonus of that trip was an excellent performance of Verdi's *Nabucco* the following night. Again conducted by Patrick Summers, the gala cast included a slightly wobbly Samuel Ramey, the sumptuous Maria Guleghina, Rafael Rojas, and Phyllis Pancella.

In August of 2000 Mimi and I traveled to Santa Fe for the combined pleasures of visiting our daughter Andy, and attending the Santa Fe Opera's five productions of that season. The trip turned out to be the most traumatic experience of my life. During intermission of the first night's *Marriage of Figaro*, Mimi came out of the restroom telling me, "You have to take me home—I'm sick, I can't see." As she said this, she sank to the ground. We managed to get her to a first-aid station, and an ambulance took her to St. Francis Hospital in the city. She was diagnosed with a massive central brainstem stroke. What probably saved her life was the early injection of blood-thinning Heparin.

She was in intensive care for several days and remained in the hospital for a week. We stayed in Patrick and Andy's house for another week while Mimi recuperated, recovering her physical and mental faculties surprisingly quickly. By the time we returned to Washington, she was walking with a walker and regaining her motor functions. Her most serious lasting disability was improper eye coordination, causing her to see double. This disability was later nearly corrected by a neuro-ophthalmologist, who placed prisms in her eyeglasses.

The episode, as I remember it, represented the nadir of my life's experience. Mimi's recovery was the start of a new life. From that point onward, everything went skyward in my appreciation and enjoyment of our life together.

We had to make some adjustments, of course. Mimi no longer drove a car, and housekeeping—cooking and shopping—fell to me. Fortunately, she regained her ability and interest in the management of our finances and bookkeeping. We were able to resume our engagement with opera, concert, theater, and movie-going and have enjoyed every moment of it.

The Glimmerglass Opera Festivals

As Mimi regained her strength and interest in new adventures, we decided in August 2001 to sample the Glimmerglass Opera Festival in Cooperstown, New York—an eight-hour drive from Washington. We had heard and read about the fine operatic productions there and had become acquainted with several Wolf Trap artists who had performed or were about to perform there. The festival exceeded our expectations, in part because we lucked into a delightful bed-and-breakfast, the Brook Willow Farm—about five miles northeast of Coopertown. The owners divided their clientele between those who come to Cooperstown to visit the Baseball Hall of Fame and those who attend the opera festival. The two groups get along well, I wish to report, in part by sharing an appreciation of the wonderful breakfast dishes created by our hostess, Chris Pohl, abetted by her husband, Bruce.

I sing the praises (no pun intended) of the B&B, where we have stayed on five subsequent visits. Its restful ambience, together with the friendly informal atmosphere of the festival, made for a real vacation in which to relax and enjoy the music presented by some highly talented artists. For sustenance, we have repeatedly returned to several excellent restaurants recommended by our hosts in and around Cooperstown.

Now to the operas, presented in one of the loveliest opera houses we have encountered. Located at the head of Glimmerglass Lake, it is an intimate, simple, airy wooden structure. It is open on the sides, but when the house darkens just before the beginning of a performance, sliding panels enclose the building (to be opened during intermission). The acoustics are excellent.

The first performance we attended was Emmanuel Chabrier's delightful operetta *L'Etoile*, conducted by Glimmerglass's musical director, Stewart Robertson. Both the singing and acting by the young cast, headed by Christine Abraham and Kevin Burdette were exemplary. Burdette was an acquaintance from the previous season at Wolf Trap.

L'Etoile was followed by an excellent production of Handel's *Agrippina*, conducted by Harry Bicket and featuring Alexandra Coku, Beth Clayton, David Walker, Karen Wierzba, and Derek Parker. The third production was Benjamin Britten's *Rape of Lucretia*, an opera I do not like—probably because the mise-en-scène was incomprehensible to me. The conductor was Stewart Robertson, and the top-notch artists were William Burden, Christine Goerke, Eric Owens, Nathan Gunn, and Michelle de Young, all known to us as Wolf Trap alumni.

The final opera was *The Marriage of Figaro* in a production we disliked because it lacked subtlety in the depiction of the sexual interplay. Musically it was a first-rate performance, led by George Manahan.

We returned to Glimmerglass the following year—as we have every year since 2001, always enjoying the relaxing yet stimulating atmosphere and experience. In 2002 we attended a beautiful production of Francis Poulenc's *Dialogues of the Carmelites*, one of my favorite twentieth-century operas. Led by Stewart Robertson, the outstanding ensemble included Maria Kanyova, the ancient Joyce Castle, Anne Evans, and Robyn Redman. Next came Haydn's delightful *Orlando Palladino*, conducted by Guido Johannes Rumstadt and featuring among other fine artists, Paul Austin Kelly and Lisa Saffer.

We skipped a performance of Adamo's *Little Women* and regretted it, thereby learning never to miss another production. The final opera of that season was the double bill of *Cavalleria Rusticana* and *Pagliacci*—in that order—in a perverse production that involved the same cast in both operas, either as soloists or as part of the chorus.

On our first evening in 2003 we attended an overproduced performance of Jacques Offenbach's *Bluebeard* in which the artists had so much stage action that they had a tough time displaying their vocal skills. Conducted by Gerald Steichen, the cast included our friend Kevin Burdette, Phyllis Pancella, Tracey Welborn, and Monica Yunus.

In one amusing episode, our B&B hostess, Chris Pohl, informed us that another guest would be Anthony Tomassini, the chief music critic of the *New York Times*. The morning after the *Bluebeard* performance he walked into the breakfast room and sat down at a table with his back to us. We had not yet been introduced. Chris came in carrying a tray of hot buns and asked me, "How was it last night?" Silently, I gave her a thumbs-down signal. She turned to Tomassini and asked him how he had liked it. Without having seen my gesture, he too gave her a thumbs-down signal. She laughed and introduced us, adding that she was glad there was agreement among her guests.

We compared assessments of the next two productions, Robert Kurka's *The Good Soldier Schweik,* and Handel's *Orlando.* We agreed on the excellence of *The Good Soldier Schweik* which was conducted by Stewart Robertson and had the outstanding Anthony Dean Griffey in the title role. Tomassini, who obviously has a much deeper understanding of the work than I, gave it a very high mark. We also shared favorable opinions of the *Orlando* production, conducted by Bernard Labadie and featuring the fine ensemble of countertenor Bejun Mehta, male soprano Michael Maniaci, sopranos Joyce Guyer and Christine Brandes, and bass David Pittsinger. Maniaci, a Wolf Trap alumnus, was the evening's real revelation—a rare male soprano with a beautifully cultivated voice and wonderful articulation.

Tomassini could not stay for the last production, *Don Giovanni,* because he had to drive up to Tanglewood that afternoon. When he told artistic director Paul Kellogg that he had to leave early, Kellogg heaved a sigh of relief, Tomassini said. We understood that sigh of relief when we attended the performance that night: it was *the* worst staging of that wonderful work—actually, of any opera—we had seen in many years. It was totally corrupted and exploited for cheap thrills. The Don was a "punker," complete with shaved head, and dressed in black leather; and his "acting" was crude and vulgar. In the final act, when the Don is supposedly swallowed up in hell, a rope dropped from the flies and the Don was pulled up into the sky. I felt like calling out that he was going in the wrong direction!

In contrast, the performance could hardly have been better vocally. Conducted by Stewart Robertson, the cast included Pall Knudsen as the Don, Kyle Ketelson as Leporello, Maria Kanyova as Donna Anna, Amy Burton as Donna Elvira, Heather Johnson as Zerlina, John McVeigh as Don Ottavio, Jeremy Gaylon as Masetto, and Gustav Andreassen as the Commendatore. I finally solved my problem by looking away from the stage and wallowing in the glorious music. I have not named the directors of most opera productions in this book, but in this case the real villain has to be identified. He was Francisco Negrin.

The 2004 season proved to be perfect. It started with Puccini's *La Fanciulla del West*, a fine production conducted by Stewart Robertson and featuring Emily Pulley (another Wolf Trap alumna) in the title role, Roger Honeywell as Dick Johnson, and Earle Patricio as the villain Jack Rance. Gilbert and Sullivan's *Patience* followed, conducted by Andrew Bisantz and featuring, among others, Sarah Coburn and Kevin Burdette, both superb Wolf Trap alumni.

Richard Rodney Bennett's *The Mines of Sulphur*, an opera first produced in London in 1965, was receiving its first professional production in the United States. It was an immediate success, both musically and dramatically. Conducted by Stewart Robertson, it had an integrated ensemble cast of first-class artists.

Our final opera that year was Handel's seldom performed *Imeneo,* in an imaginative production conducted by William Lacey. It featured again the superb young male soprano, Michael Maniaci, in a cast of fine singers.

Mimi had another serious physical mishap—a new medical condition—in the spring of 2004 that nearly caused us to cancel the entire season. The previous summer she had begun to take frequent falls on her daily walks and really hurt herself on one of these falls. On the advice of our family physician we consulted a neurologist. He diagnosed Mimi with hydrocephalus, an excess of spinal fluid pressing on the brain, and referred her to the Adult Hydrocephalus Clinic at Johns Hopkins University in Baltimore. The clinic's director, Dr. David Williams, advised her after extensive tests that in his opinion the surgery that had been scheduled might be premature, as her symptoms did not appear so serious. He suggested, however, that should she feel the need at some point, they would perform the surgery—an implantation of a shunt in her brain to relieve the pressure causing her symptoms.

With this advice Mimi decided to postpone the operation. Then, in May of the following year, 2004, she fell down the stairs in our house and injured her back so badly that she was literally unable to use her legs. It took a week in the hospital and five weeks in rehab to enable her to walk again—initially with some difficulty, using a walker at first, and then a cane with assistance from me. That was the situation when we went to Glimmerglass that August. Mimi was able to manage the trip and enjoy the operas. We had made some adjustments in our theater seating arrangements and in our B&B accommodations to keep her comfortable.

The hydrocephalus surgery which had been rescheduled as soon as she was able to maneuver her legs again took place that September. It turned out to be a miraculous success: six hours after the surgery Mimi was able to walk down the hospital hall with confidence, without anyone's help, and using her cane only for insurance. Her gait was normal. Gone was the shuffle that is symptomatic of hydrocephalus. Mimi was literally a rejuvenated person, both physically and mentally; her recovery was total.

Thus our pilgrimage to Glimmerglass in 2005 was, once again, a real vacation. Musically the season was good, if not perfect. The first production, Benjamin Britten's *Death in Venice,* is an opera that, on first hearing, a lay person can admire but not enjoy. It is an extremely difficult work to understand both mucially and dramatically, and it takes a real effort to comprehend its worth as a musical creation. Conducted by Stewart Robertson, William Burden was a superb vocal interpreter in the leading role of Aschenbach.

Completely successful, in our view, was Donizetti's *Lucia de Lammermoor,* sung in its French version. Conducted by Beatrice Jona Affron, the title role was performed beautifully by Sarah Coburn, both vocally and dramatically, notwithstanding Anne Midgette's carping in the *New York Times* about her inadequate French.

Next came one of those incomprehensible, idiosyncratic productions of *Cosi fan Tutte* for which Glimmerglass is occasionally known. Once again I shall single out the director, Tim Albery, for derision. He set the opera in a huge square contraption—which I learned later was supposed to resemble an old box camera—that opened to reveal the action of the opera. Led by Stewart Robertson, the saving grace was a delightful ensemble cast of artists mostly unknown to me—Anne Sophie Duprels as Fiordiligi, Sandra Pique Eddy as Dorabella, Camille Zamora as Despina, John Tessier as Ferrando, Palle Knudsen (the punk Don Giovanni from 2003) as Guglielmo, and Sanford Sylvan as Alfonso.

The last production was a double bill: Poulenc's *La Voix Humaine,* a one-person tour de force sung by the excellent Amy Burton, and Massenet's *Le Portrait de Manon* which on first hearing I considered a trifle.

Our sixth visit to Glimmerglass, in 2006, was such a good season I must report on our experience one more time. The weather was great—bright sunshine and warm temperatures during the day, and cool nights (though not as cold as a previous occasion when we needed blankets to stay warm during the performance). Having been ridiculed by friends over five years for never having visited the Baseball Hall of Fame, for which Cooperstown is most famed throughout the country, we spent a couple of hours in this impressive museum and can now tell the world that we have been there.

The Glimmerglass festival remains, however, our only reason for making the annual trek to Cooperstown, and we were rewarded with four performances, three of them pure joy. The fourth production, the world premiere of Stephen Hartke's *The Greater Good, or, the Passion of Boule de Suif*, based quite literally on the famous Guy de Maupassant short story "Boule de Suif," resulted in a rarely divided view between Mimi and me. Mimi did not like it at all and was quite bored by it. I shared her view of the music but felt that on first hearing—despite having read about the composition and heard an introductory lecture on the opera—it was my untrained ear and my inability to comprehend Hartke's aesthetic that caused me to be put off by the composition. But I was intrigued by the production—the staging of the drama—and particularly the characterization of the title character, Boule de Suif, by the impressive soprano Caroline Worra.[19]

We saw *The Greater Good* on our first night, so that Rossini's *Barber of Seville*, which came next, could not have been a greater musical and comedic contrast. Directed by Leon Major, this was my sixteenth *Barber*, and I can't remember a production as delightful musically, visually, comically, imaginatively, or as a performance—a perfectly executed evening! Led by David Angus, the orchestra played superbly, and the ensemble was musically and dramatically impeccable (if that is what you can call a fun fest). All of them—Aaron St.Clair as the barber, Katharine Goldner as Rosina, John Tessier as Almaviva, Eduardo Chama as Dr. Bartolo, Daniel Sumegi as Basilio, and, not to forget, Judith Christin as Berta, and Steven Walker as the ever-silent Ambrogio—made for an ensemble *sans pareil*.

The *Barber* was followed by a revelatory production of Leos Janáček's *Jenufa*. Directed by the noted Jonathan Miller, the opera was dramatically and vocally both inspiring and exciting, especially the singing of the two women—Maria Kanyova in the title role and Elizabeth Byrne as Kostelnicka. Led by Stewart Robertson in his final appearance as music director of the Glimmerglass Opera Company, the orchestra again played as an equal partner with the fine ensemble, which also included Judith Christin as the grandmother, Roger Honeywell as Laca, and Scott Piper as Steva.

The final production of the summer was Gilbert and Sullivan's *Pirates of Penzance*. Conducted by Gary Thor Wedow, it was a typically fine, humorous Glimmerglass ensemble endeavor, well sung and well played for the enjoyment of all.

The Met, the New York City Opera, the Kirov Opera, and the Kennedy Center

In addition to our regularly scheduled opera subscription series in Washington and Cooperstown, we attended a number of particularly memorable performances in recent years that need to be recorded here.

In March 2003 we attended three extraordinary performances at the Metropolitan Opera in New York. First came Berlioz's *Benvenuto Cellini*, conducted by James Levine in an idiosyncratic production that featured Marcello Giordano in the title role, Isabel Bayrakdarin, John del Carlo, Kristine Jepson, and Robert Lloyd. Next came Jacques Halevy's *La Juive*, conducted by Marcello Viotti. Neil Shicoff sang the title role in a fine characterization and with still acceptable, if not great, voice. He was joined by a superior cast, including Soile Isokoski, whom we had not heard before, the always delightful Elizabeth Futral, Eric Cutler, and Feruccio Furlanetto.

The third opera on that trip, and possibly the *pièce de resistance*, was a fabulous production of Richard Strauss's *Die Frau ohne Schatten*. Conducted by Philippe Auguin, it was a star turn for Deborah Voigt, a performance I will not forget. The Met orchestra and the other artists—Deborah Polanski, Jane Henschel, Wolfgang Brendel, and Mark Delavan—formed a brilliant ensemble.

The Kirov Opera from St. Petersburg came to the Kennedy Center in Washington in the late fall of 2003 and presented two operas by Tchaikovsky—the ubiquitous *Eugene Onegin* and Washington's first hearing of *Mazeppa*,. Both were conducted by Valery Gergiev. *Eugene Onegin* was impressively sung by Evgeny Nikitin, Elena Lasovskaya, Natalya Evstafyeva, Evgeny Akimov, and Mikhail Kit. *Mazeppa* featured Nikolai Putilin and Tatiana Pavlovskaya, both well known in Washington, and Oleg Balashov.

We made another pilgrimage to New York in the spring of 2005 to hear Handel's *Orlando* at the New York City Opera, and Verdi's *Don Carlo* and *Un Ballo in Maschera* at the Met. The *Orlando* production was the same we had heard in 2003 at Glimmerglass, where the setting was much more intimate and musically attractive. The opera was well conducted by Antony Walker, the music director of the Washington Concert Opera making his debut at the New York City Opera, and featured a cast that, with the exception of Bejun Mehta and David Pittsinger, differed from that at Glimmerglass but was equally good: Jennifer Aylmer, Amy Burton, and Matthew White.

At the Met we seemed to hit an operatic jackpot. *Don Carlo*, ably led in its full five-act version by Fabio Luisi, a conductor new to us, featured a stellar cast of Eduardo Villa in the title role, Sondra Radvanovsky—a revelation as Elisabet—Violeta Urmana as Eboli, Dwayne Croft as Rodrigo, Ferrucio Furlanetto as Philip, and Paata Burchuladze as the Grand Inquisitor.

Un Ballo in Maschera, led by the always fine James Conlon, featured a newly svelte Deborah Voigt in glorious voice. She was joined by Marcello Giordano, Carlos Alvarez, Marianne Cornetti, and Lyubov Petrova in a superb ensemble cast.

To end this chapter on a beautiful note, I report on a spectacular performance by Renee Fleming, singing the title role of Daphne in the seldom performed Richard Strauss opera of the same name, in a concert version at Washington's Kennedy Center in October 2005. Semyon Bychkov conducted the WDR Symphony Orchestra of Cologne in this tour de force, and all I can say is that, although we have had the opportunity to hear Renee Fleming on several memorable occasions, I know I shall never forget this one.

15

The Wolf Trap Experience

Finally, and on a happy note, I write about our appreciation of and involvement with the Wolf Trap Opera Company in Vienna, Virginia, just outside of Washington.

It all started in the summer of 1986, when we were persuaded to attend a performance of Offenbach's *Tales of Hoffmann* in the huge Filene Center, the main performance venue of the Wolf Trap Foundation for the Performing Arts. Known as the Shed, it accommodates an audience of thousands, (As mentioned earlier, we had heard an opera at Wolf Trap once before, in 1978, when we attended the world premiere of Stephen Douglas Burton's *The Duchess of Malfi*.)

What was unforgettable about this performance was Tracy Dahl, singing the role of the doll Olympia. While brilliantly trilling her stratospheric coloratura aria, she crossed the huge stage on roller skates, perfectly stiff and still, not moving a visible muscle—back and forth, back and forth. It brought down the house, and to this day it produces an admiring headshake whenever I think of it.

We were hooked! From then on, and until this day, we have attended every opera performance of the Wolf Trap Opera Company, with one exception, for a total so far of fifty-nine productions.

By way of explanation, the Wolf Trap Opera Company (WTOC) performs two operas during the summer months in the Barns and one in the Shed. The Barns, a small, 382-seat, acoustically excellent wooden theater with a small stage and a tiny orchestra pit, is suitable for baroque or classical music productions (Handel, Mozart, Rossini, Donizetti) and some contemporary works. The Barns is the opera company's principal venue. Its director, Kim Pensinger Witman, holds yearly nationwide auditions for over three hundred young artists on the cusp of their professional careers. An average of fifteen are chosen to spend three months studying, rehearsing, and performing the repertory. Only after Kim has selected the program's participants does she decide on the three operas to be performed the following summer—two in the Barns, one in the Shed. In other words, the operas are chosen on the basis of the selected talent, rather than the other way around, so that the repertory is matched to the available voices and artistic temperaments. The results have been musically and theatrically outstanding, and a large number of the singing artists have gone on to become renowned stars of the current worldwide opera stages.

In an article in the August 1993 issue of the *Foreign Service Journal* entitled "The Coming of Age of Washington Opera," I wrote that the Wolf Trap Opera Company "has come to fill a necessary role as a sort of U.S. farm team for the big league of international opera—a service to young American artists, in view of the fact that the United States, unlike Europe, has only a few high-quality provincial opera houses with extensive seasons and large repertories to perform this apprentice function. In some respects the WTOC resembles the physical and musical ambiance of the Glyndebourne Festival in England in the 1950s—let's say a bourgeois Glyndebourne; in other respects it is an uncomplicated rustic equivalent of Santa Fe's famed festival. With both it has in common exquisite musical taste and sophistication."

As recently as November 2005, Anne Midgette wrote a rather critical article in the *New York Times* about the dearth of good training of American opera singers. In response, I wrote an unpublished letter to the editor pointing out that while the Wolf Trap venue is not suitable for the production of highly dramatic operas and limits itself to works by composers such as Purcell, Handel, Mozart, Rossini, and the more contemporary Britten, Floyd, Sondheim, and Musto, the list of Wolf Trap alumni who go on to success on the world's major opera stages is getting longer every year. It includes, among many others, Dawn Upshaw, Richard Croft, Denyce Graves, John Aler, Tracy Dahl, Mark Delavan, David Kuebler, Eric Cutler, Charlotte Hellekant, Elizabeth Futral, Paul Groves, Heidi Grant Murphy, Mary Dunleavy, Nathan Gunn, Mel Ulrich, Christine Goerke, Emily Pulley, Marie Plette, Michael Maniaci, Larry Brownlee, Patricia Risley, Keith Phares, Michelle de Young, and even the "Wagnerians" Alan Held, Gordon Hawkins, Margaret Jane Wray, and Stephanie Blythe.

And now to the actual performances. Again, I shall confine myself to writing about those performances and artists sticking in my memory, but even with that self-imposed limitation, there are many that I consider as unforgettable as that initial *Tales of Hoffmann*. Most of these performances were in the Barns.

In 1987, it was Carlisle Floyd's *Susannah* (a production of the Prince George's Civic Opera), and Cavalli's *L'Ormindo*, our first hearing of both of these fine operas, whose composers lived three hundred years apart. Next (in the Shed) came the most impressive production of Britten's *Midsummer Night's Dream* that we have ever attended. Richard Woitach conducted, and among the performing artists were Drew Minter, Margaret Jane Wray, Paul Austin Kelly, and Alan Held.

In 1988 we heard two other operas new to us: Stravinsky's *Rape of Lucretia*, conducted by Cal Stewart Kellogg, and Prokofiev's *Love for Three Oranges*, conducted by Vjekoslav Sutej. Margaret Jane Wray sang in both of them, and Alan Held and Peter Volpe sang in the Prokofiev

In 1989 Purcell's *Dido and Aeneas* was new to us, with Heidi Grant Murphy and Denyce Graves in small roles making their stage debuts. In the same year we heard Dawn Upshaw for the first time, singing Susannah in *The Marriage of Figaro*. A consummate musician with such a lovely voice, Upshaw had returned for an encore appearance after being a WTOC artist the year before we returned to Washington. Heidi Grant Murphy and Denyce Graves also sang in that performance.

In 1990 we heard two Rossini operas for the first time. One, *Journey to Reims*, conducted by Steven Mercurio, included all 1990 WTOC artists in singing roles. The other, *L'Italiana in Algeri*, conducted by George Manahan, featured Phyllis Pancella, among others.

In 1991 we heard Cimarosa's delightful *Il Matrimonio Secreto*, conducted by Kellogg and featuring Charles Workman, Elizabeth Futral, Marianne Cornetti, Marie Caruso, and Raymond Aceto; and an equally enchanting *Marriage of Figaro*, conducted by Hal France, and introducing Charlotte Hellekant to us.

The 1992 season brought our first *La Finta Giardiniera* by Mozart conducted by Will Crutchfield, featuring William Burden among the fine ensemble cast. And in 1993 we heard two less frequently performed operas. Rossini's *A Turk in Italy was* conducted by Yves Abel, and introduced Mary Dunleavy and Mel Ulrich to us. Mozart's *La Clemenza di Tito* was conducted by Stephen Lord and featured Marie Plette and Nancy Maultsby, among other fine artists.

The 1994 Mozart anniversary year brought two works by the composer and one quasi-Mozart opera, *The Jewel Box*, a concoction of music by Wolfgang Amadeus, assembled with a new storybook by Paul Griffiths. The genuine Mozart operas were *Cosi fan tutte*, conducted by John Keenan, and *The Magic Flute*, conducted by Yves Abel. These operas introduced Yvonne Gonzalez, Nathan Gunn, Margaret Lattimore, Eric Owens, and Emily Pulley.

The year 1995 was notable for presenting young artists who went on to greater things, to wit, Stephanie Blythe (whose Tisbe in *Cenerentola* and Fidalma in *I1 Matrimonio Secreto* I will never forget), Michelle de Young, Christine Goerke, Yvonne Gonsalez, Nathan Gunn, Margaret Lattimore, Eric Owens, Steven Condy, and Emily Pulley. That year we also heard our second *Julio Caesar*, conducted by Patrick Summer, compensating for that atrocious production we suffered through in Frankfurt.

In 1996 we again heard *Il Viaggio à Reims* by Rossini, conducted by Stephen Lord, and *Falstaff*, the first Verdi opera, presented at Wolf Trap. Conducted by Stephen Beckwith, *Falstaff* featured Steven Condy in the title role, and introduced Jennifer Aylmer and Gregory Turay among others.

In 1997 we were introduced to three operas we had never heard before: A double bill of Rossini's *La Cambiale de Matrimonio* and *L'occasione fa il ladro*, both conducted by Massimiliano Stefanelli, and Mozart's early *Mitridate*, conducted by Antony Walker, who subsequently became music director of the Washington Concert Opera. Among the new young artists that year were Nicole Heaston, Patricia Risley, Meagan Miller and Leslie Johnson.

The 1998 season featured a new *Cosi fan tutte*, conducted by Christopher Larkin; *The Abduction from the Seraglio*, conducted by Stephen Beckwith; and Rossini's *Barber of Seville*. In 1999 we heard Mozart's *Idomeneo*, conducted by Antony Walker; Stravinsky's *The Rake's Progress*, conducted by Stephen Crout, then the music director of the Washington Concert Opera; and a new production of *The Magic Flute*, conducted by Scott Bergeson. John Marcus Bindel, Justin Vickers, Jennifer Welch, and Daniel Belcher were among the young artists introduced during those two years.

In 2000 the WTOC produced the rarely presented Monteverdi opera *L'incoronazione di Poppea*, conducted by David Fallis. It featured Anna Christy, Keith Phares, Cynthia Walters, and Joshua Winograde, and introduced the young male soprano Michael Maniaci, whom I will mention in more detail later. The other production that year was Rossini's *L'Italiana in Algeri*, conducted by J. David Jackson, with Jossie Perez, Keith Phares and Joshua Winograde.

The summer of 2001 brought two novelties in one evening, Mozart's *Impresario* and Donizetti's *Viva la mama*, and was followed by a lovely production of Benjamin Britten's *Midsummernight's Dream*, conducted by Jane Glover and introducing Adriana Zabala, Lauren Skuce, Oren Gradus, Justin Vickers, and Lawrence Brownlee. Our close friends Sheila and Bill Woessner hosted Brownlee during his stay that summer, and we got to know him on a personal basis.

His exposure in the two productions that summer was rather limited, so that we only began to admire this phenomenal artist and his beautiful lyric tenor voice in subsequent hearings. I will come back to Larry Brownlee later in this chapter.

During 2002 Mimi and I switched from being mere fans of the WTOC to becoming supporters, as members of the Catherine Filene Shouse Legacy Circle. Thus, I suppose, my critical faculties may be considered somewhat compromised. But I shall try in this report to continue living up to high—albeit amateur—critical standards when writing about this fine organization.

The 2002 season turned out fascinating. It started with a production of Donizetti's *Don Pasquale*, conducted by Dean Williamson, that featured two of our favorite male singers, Kevin Burdette as the Don, and Ryan Taylor as Dr. Malatesta. The young Ross Hauck and Angela Gilbert completed the delightful ensemble. Next came a memorable production of Handel's *Xerxes*, conducted by Gary Thor Widow. It featured male soprano Michael Maniaci in the title role. His singing revealed what a beautiful, well-trained, and now mature high male voice can accomplish. Maniaci was surrounded by a near-perfect ensemble—Stacy Richoi, Angela Fout, Adriana Zabala, Miranda Row, and Kevin Burdette.

The season ended in the Shed with a major novelty—a production of Kurt Weil's *Street Scene*, conducted by Richard Bado. While *Street Scene* opened and ran on Broadway in the 1950s, it is in every respect a contemporary opera. It was a major endeavor, scenically, dramatically, and musically, and a total success, involving the entire opera company and then some. It was also a financial disaster for the company, forcing Kim Witman and her Wolf Trap Foundation colleagues to rethink how to present in the Shed only operas sufficiently popular to attract the large audience required for this venue.

In the 2003 season came my single disappointing WTOC experience, a failed production of Mozart's *La Clemenza di Tito*. I suppose such a disapointment had to come at some time, and this one was pretty total. I had seen the opera only a couple of times before, in 1993 here at Wolf Trap, and in 1995 at the famed Semper Oper in Dresden, in a performance that was beautifully sung and acted and delightfully produced. This 2003 WTOC production was set in the mid-1920s with horrible costumes. The female artists in trouser roles all wore ill-fitting garments that made me want to exclaim, "Sam, you made the pants too long!" Although well conducted by Steven Mosteller, the production was hampered by the inadequate singing of Simon O'Neil in the role of the emperor, physically compromised by a huge imitation brass eagle breastplate attached to his costume. The fine artistry of Carolyn Betty, Stacey Rishoi, Miranda Rowe, and Angela Niederloh somewhat compensated for the rest of the production.

What saved the season was a delightful production of the rarely performed *Dardanus* by Jean Philippe Rameau. Conducted by Antony Walker, the cast included Marie Lenormand, whose native French diction was a real asset to her singing and interpretation. The production of *The Barber of Seville*, a dependable crowd pleaser performed in the Shed, was conducted by Dean Williamson, and introduced two superb artists: Sarah Coburn in the role of Rosina and Matt Boehler as Basilio.

In the spring of 2004, the WTOC produced the first opera it had commissioned, *Volpone*, by John Musto and the librettist Mark Campbell. In preparation for over three years, the work was a true collaborative effort under the leadership of Kim Witman. Conducted by Michael Barrett, and directed by Leon Major, the cast consisted of five WTOC alumni: bass Joshua Winograde ('00 and '01) in the title role of the fox; mezzo Adriana Zabala ('01 and '02) as Erminella the ermine; Ryan Taylor ('01 and '02) as Voltore the vulture; tenor Ross Hauck ('02 and '03) as Bonari; and soprano Sara Wolfson ('01) as Celia. They were joined by tenor Jason Ferrante as Cornaccio the crow, tenor Joseph Kaiser as Mosca the fly, and soprano Wendy Hill as Corvina the raven.

The production was a singular success. I will let the *Wall Street Journal* (March 24, 2004) speak for the critical evaluation:

> [Composer John Musto's and librettist Mark Campbell's] *Volpone* "unfaithfully based" on Ben Johnson's play...is an effervescent black comedy. With swift, tightly rhymed, funny text, impeccably set to contrapuntal, singable vocal lines interwoven with a lightly scored orchestration brimming with comic touches, the piece is witty, unsentimental and thoroughly engaging...Each act builds to a riotous ensemble, worthy successor to those famous Rossini finales, yet with contemporary sonic palette.

My one quibble, known to the opera's producers, was the regrettable absence of surtitles which, in my view, were needed to enhance comprehension of the witty libretto. It was impossible to understand the hilarious text, so fittingly integrated with the music, especially when sung by female voices and ensembles. And that is a pity, since the opera thereby loses some of its ingenious creative sheen. It was my hope that the opera would be revived in an early

Adriana Zabala and Joshua Winograde singing in the John Musto–Mark Campbell world premiere production of their opera Volpone, *commissioned by the Wolf Trap Opera Company in 2004 (Wolf Trap Opera).*

coming season with surtitles. It deserves repeated hearing and belongs in the repertory of contemporary chamber operas.[20]

The 2004 summer season brought another novelty, Antonio Salieri's comic opera, *Falstaff*—musically quite different from Verdi's masterpiece but certainly delightful and deserving to be heard. Conducted by Steven Mosteller, it featured Brian Mulligan as the title character and Laquita Mitchell, Jason Hardy, Marcus Beam, Angela Niederloh, Dimitri Pittas, and Kristin Reiersen in the other roles.

And 2005 featured another landmark event, the company's first venture into what is commonly known as musical comedy, Stephen Sondheim's *Sweeney Todd*. This ingenious musical/dramatic creation certainly qualifies as contemporary opera and has been performed in some major U.S. opera houses. It received an outstanding operatic production in the hands of conductor James Lowe,, director Joe Banno, and the young cast. Sweeney Todd was sung by Mark Boehler ,another fine singing actor who will go far in the opera world, as will Jason Hardy, who sang the role of Judge Turpin.

Other members of the cast, who all contributed most effectively to this ensemble production, were Audrey Babcock as Mrs. Lovett, Jason Ferrante as Beadle, Javier Abreu as Tobias Ragg, Nicholas Phan as Pirelli, Maureen McKay as Johanna, and Alexander Tall as Anthony Hope.

Again, my one regret was the absence of surtitles. I happen to have seen *Sweeney Todd* three times before in the theater and was familiar with the text, but many in the audience—including friends who were with me—missed much of the integral story line because they could not understand the unmiked artists, especially the female voices and vocal ensembles. The audience's appreciation of this fine musical creation was thereby handicapped.

A beautiful chamber production of *Don Giovanni* elicited a note from me to Kim Witman, in which I commented that I had seen the opera twenty-two times before, of which five stood out in my memory. The first two were Furtwängler's at Salzburg in 1950 and 1951, and the third, Solti's at Glyndebourne in 1954. The fourth, while musically excellent, was the memorably disgusting production at Glimmerglass in 2003. And the fifth was this impressive WTOC chamber production, wherein the music and drama were fully integrated and the voices and dramatization uniformly excellent. Ari Pelto conducted, Ned Canby directed, and the cast consisted of Brian Mulligan in the title role, Matt Boehler as Leporello, Marjorie Owens as Donna Anna, Laquita Mitchell as Donna Elvira, Evelyn Pollock as Zerlina, Jason Hardy as the Commendatore, Norman Reinhardt as Don Ottavio, and Daniel Gross as Masetto.

Necessity was the mother of invention in the 2006 presentation of *Cenerentola* in the Shed. Budgetary limitations forced the producers to eliminate the elaborate scenery and to stage the opera in front of the orchestra in a modified concert version. It proved a singular success. A major factor of this success was Dean Williamson's sensitive conducting, keeping the National Symphony Orchestra on stage in balance with the artists in front of them. Equally responsible for this delightful production was the stage direction by Garnett Bruce, who made the nonexistent scenery superfluous, and created hilarious shenanigans on the lip of the stage without ever detracting from the musical values of the opera. And the artists, led by the delightful young mezzo coloratura Kate Lindsay in the title role, sang and acted their hearts out, giving new meaning to this comic masterpiece. Since they all shared in the success of this production, they will be named here also: Javier Abreu as Don Ramiro, the excruciatingly funny Evelyn Pollock and Audrey Babcock as the two sisters, Clorinda and Tisbe, Jason Hardy as Don Magnifico, Weston Hurst as Dandini, and Daniel Gross as Alidoro.

As the last opera performance entries in this chapter I want to discuss briefly three productions in the 2006 season that were unusual in many respects. The first was a presentation of *Orpheus,* by the early eighteenth-century composer Georg Phillipp Telemann. To the best of my knowledge, it had never before been performed in this country. Kim Witman, WTOC's director, had long valued this composition and had been waiting for the right ensemble to put it in an innovative production, warranted because the Orpheus story depicted in this opera is quite different from the well-known tale.

Witman's success was complete. Conducted by the excellent Guido Rumstadt (the same Guido Rumstadt I had encountered in Frankfurt in 1995 conducting *Lady Macbeth of Mtsensk* and again at Glimmerglass in 2002 conducting Haydn's *Orlando Palladino*), the ensemble included Alex Tall in the title role, Browen Forbay in the stratospherically placed role of Orasia, Fiona Murphy as Euridice, and Jeremy Little, Evelyn Pollock, Maureen McKay, Matt Boehler, and Ronnita Miller. It was a beautifully sung and well-acted performance.

The second 2006 opera in the Barns was Rossini's *Le Comte Ory*. Kim Witman had this seldom performed comedy in mind for several years and had actually planned it for the 2002 season, having found a qualified high lyric tenor for the title role in Larry Brownlee. But La Scala in Milan offered Brownlee the role of Almaviva in *The Barber of Seville,* an offer he could not refuse, thus ruling out his return to Wolf Trap for *Le Comte Ory* that summer. Witman eventually found a similarly qualified tenor in Javier Abreu (he had been at Wolf Trap the previous year in the role of Ramiro in *Cenerentola*), and so this delightful opera found a venue at Wolf Trap. The conductor was Robert Wood, and the talented and marvellously rehearsed ensemble included, besides Abreu, Lauren McNeese as Isolier, Heidi Stober as Countess Adele, Ronnita Miller as Ragonde, Museop Kim as Raimbaud, Faith Sherman as Alice, and Ryan McKinny as Gouverneur. It ws a sprightly and expertly executed music show.

After the successful experience with Rossini's *Cenerentola* in the Filene Center in 2005, the Opera Company presented a semistaged version of Gounod's *Romeo et Juliet* on the huge stage of the Shed in July 2006. With the National Symphony Orchestra on stage, the "action," ingeniously directed by Ellen Douglas Schlaefer, took place in front of the orchestra, performed by an ensemble trained to perfection. Led by the highly respected Stephen Lord, the orchestra and vocal artists were integrated and balanced; not an easy task, as the singers had to be amplified so that they could be heard not only in the large shed but also on the hilly lawn behind the Shed where hundreds of viewers sat in the grass.

Romeo was sung by Chad Freeburg, Juliet by the sparkling Ailyn Perez. They were joined by the excellent ensemble of Alexander Tall as Mercutio, Jason Ferrante as Tybalt, Matt Boehler as Frere Laurent and Le Duc, Fiona Murphy as Stephano, Museop Kim as Capulet, Faith Sherman as Gertrude, Weston Hurt as Paris and Gregorio, and Jeremy Little as Benvolio.

In May 2003, the Wolf Trap Foundation had dedicated its newly built Center for Education, a lovely state-of-the-art educational resource center located in the woods next to the Barns. Mimi and I decided to donate my extensive collection of opera, concert, and theater programs—some dating back to the 1930s and 1940s and totaling around 2500 items—plus our collection of opera and concert scores, videotapes, LPs, audio tapes, and CDs to serve as the basis of a music library and archive. The collection has been catalogued and computerized and now serves as a much used database.

Kim Witman, who has been the WTOC's director since 1997, assumed the additional duties of director of classical programming at Wolf Trap in 2006. With her remarkable musical and managerial expertise, she has created further opportunities for her young opera artists to demonstrate their talents during the summer months. Artistically, the most valuable of these have been the two vocal recitals organized and presented by Steven Blier each summer since 1995. Blier, the renowned musicologist and pianist, who has programmed, performed, and annotated over ninety vocal recitals for the New York Festival of Song as its cofounder and director, spends a couple of weeks each summer at Wolf Trap, working with the young vocal artists. In two groups of three to five, these young artists present recitals that Blier introduces and accompanies. Performed in the intimate Barns under unifying themes with titles, such as "Where the Boys Are" and "The Latest Word" in 2005, they are considered by both the participating singers and the appreciative audiences to be highpoints of the summer musical season.

In the summer of 2007, one of the two recitals was entitled "Berlin Night Life," with soprano Bronwen Forbay, mezzo-soprano Kate Lindsey, tenor Rodell Rosel, and bass Marc Webster. Blier had selected songs by Kurt Weil and other celebrated German song composers, and he "drilled" the young artists in the distinctive Berlin cabaret style and pronounced Berlin dialect for their performances. Most of these cabaret songs were probably unfamiliar to an American audience, but for me they were hometown music that brought forth a moment's nostalgia. All four artists were terrific, but I must mention especially Kate Lindsey, the young mezzo, who is now singing featured roles at the Met. In her body language, her expressive Berlin dialect, and her smoky yet lovely voice, she personified the 1930s' Berlin cabaret singer to perfection.

During the last few years, Kim Witman herself has presented recitals with several of her WTOC alumni. Thus, in 2001, she accompanied Mel Ulrich and, in 2002, Megan Miller. In 2003, Kim accompanied Adriana Zabala and Ryan Taylor in a memorable presentation of Hugo Wolf's *Italienisches Liederbuch*, and in 2004 she accompanied Jennifer Aylmer in a recital entitled, "Songs of Our Youth."

In 2005, Whitman accompanied WTOC alumnus Nathan Gunn in Schubert's *Die Schöne Müllerin*, an outstandingly beautiful recital that fully justified Gunn's rise into the foremost ranks of current lyric baritones. Anthony Tommasini wrote in the *New York Times* (January 8, 2006) that, "by any measure this is a breakout season for...Nathan Gunn at the Metropolitan...Mr. Gunn represents a new generation of college-trained American vocal artists: top notch musicians who both sing with honesty and are adventurous actors who throw themselves into roles and care about their looks."

(Incidentally, while Kim travels on her annual audition tour, she produces a daily blog that has become a useful guide to those around the country auditioning for the WTOC and other opera venues. Her daily ruminations about her auditioning chores have certainly taught me how little I know about the art of singing!)

I can not end this chapter without writing about another WTOC alumnus, our friend, Larry Brownlee. During the last four years he has been singing lyrical tenor roles at La Scala and other leading European opera houses. In January 2006 he gave a recital (accompanied by Howard Watkins) at the Kennedy Center under the auspices of the Vocal Arts Society. Tim Page in the *Washington Post* (January 7, 2006) described Larry's recital as follows:

> Listening to Lawrence Brownlee sing...is a little bit like falling into a time warp. Most of the tenors to whom this spectacularly gifted young Ohioan can profitably be compared flourished the better part of a century ago... Brownlee summons to mind the recordings made by the generation before Caruso—Italian tenors such as Fernando de Lucia and Alessandro Bonci, with their Old World suavity, their dazzling and cultivated vocal agility, their caressing emphasis on unbroken lyrical sweetness.... A real live coloratura tenor in the all-but-forgotten grand manner,...his scales are bright and fluid, his pitch sense is

spot-on and his moderate-size but powerful and distinctive voice assumes a haunting pathos in softer passages.

Brownlee came back to Washington again in April 2006 to sing with the Washington Concert Opera in Rossini's *Tancredi*, in the company of two other WTOC alumnae, the now famed mezzo diva Stephanie Blythe and the newly crowned coloratura star Sarah Coburn. And in April 2007, Larry finally made his debut at the Metropolitan Opera, appearing as Almaviva in *The Barber of Seville*. Anthony Tommassini wrote in the *New York Times* (May 5, 2007) that Brownlee is "an appealing stage performer with a bright, sweet and flexible voice [who] made a strong impression and won a warm ovation."

Larry Brownlee making his debut at the Met as Almaviva in Rossini's Barber of Seville *(Ken Howard).*

Postlude

Since I began my life with music in Berlin, I also want to end the story of this odyssey there. In November 2006 I was invited to participate in the sixtieth anniversary of the founding of the German-American Institute, the America House, in Nuremberg. I accepted on the condition that I could spend a couple of days in Berlin. I had not been in my native city since it had once again become Germany's capital, and I wanted to see some of the new things that had been added to the cityscape in the subsequent fifteen years.

My hotel was centrally located on Friedrichstrasse, one block from Unter Den Linden, and only a few blocks from Kronenstrasse 16, my birthplace. (A large office building is now in its place.)

Next door to the hotel is the Komische Oper, where I witnessed the positively worst opera production of my life. It was *Madama Butterfly*, set in a contemporary bordello where Butterfly, a resident, demonstrated a number of sexual acts and positions. At the end, she kills her child, her attendant Suzuki, and her "husband" Pinkerton. Walter Felsenstein, the legendary director of the Komische Oper, mentioned earlier in this book, would turn over in his grave were he aware of this flagrant travesty on the art of opera. Enough said!

In compensation, I attended a delightful matinee recital in the Staatsoper by Daniel Barenboim and the soprano Dorothea Röschmann, performing two Liederkreise by Robert Schumann in commemoration of the 150th anniversary of the composer's death. What a fine musical experience!

Though that performance was hard to top, I attended an equally memorable concert that same evening by the Berlin Philharmonic, playing Shostakovich's First and Fifteenth Symphonies under the superb direction of Sir Simon Rattle, its musical director. Having attended almost weekly concerts in the Philharmonie during our residency in Berlin in the late 1960s, I was surprised on this occasion to be almost overwhelmed by the totality of the musical experience that I felt anew in this remarkable auditorium.

I made it my business to see in those two days the major new architectural features that had changed Berlin's appearance. Among these were the Holocaust Memorial, the Jewish Museum, and the rebuilt Reichstag, with its huge glass dome that delivered an impressive 360-degree view of the city's center.

As I absorbed this panoramic view of the city of my birth, I felt that my diplomatic career had indeed come full circle. But my musical apreciation had by no means reached its coda. I expect that arias and cabalettas will continue to enrich my life with Mimi, even if unrecorded here.

Notes

[1] The author's collection of approximately 2,500 opera, concert, recital, and theater programs now resides in the music library and archive of the Wolf Trap Foundation in Vienna, Virginia. The collection is catalogued on the library's computer and is available for verification and additional information.

[2] Angela Möller, "*Die Gründung der Amerika Häuser 1945–1949*," MA dissertation (unpublished), Ludwig-Maximilians Universität München, 1984, p 159.

[3] New York: Alfred A. Knopf, 1966.

[4] Sir Georg Solti, *Memoirs* (New York: Alfred Knopf, 1997).

[5] See Hans N. Tuch, *Communicating with the World: U.S. Public Diplomacy Overseas* (New York: St. Martin's Press, 1990), 18–19.

[6] For an explanation of the workings and results of this agreement, see Tuch, *Communicating with the World*, 124-139.

[7] Norris Houghton, *Return Engagment* (New York: Holt, Rinehart & Winston, 1962).

[8] I first reported this story in an article entitled "Surviving the Cold War" in the *Foreign Service Journal*, February 1998.

[9] The *New York Times* published a story on July 22, 2005, about the appointment of Paula Rosenberg as *Intendant* of the Berlin Philharmonic, describing her as "the first American to hold the position." I wrote a letter to the editor pointing out that this was incorrect, that Wolfgang Stresemann, although of German birth (he was the son of Gustav Stresemann, Germany's foreign minister in the Weimar Republic), was an American citizen when he served as *Intendant* of the Berlin Philharmonic. The *Times* finally acknowledged the mistake in their "Corrections" Column on January 22, 2006.

[10] Max Frankel, *The Times of My Life and My Life with the Times* (New York: Random House, 1994), 501.

[11] "Practicing Public Diplomacy in Brazil," in Tuch, *Communicating with the World*, 140–51.

[12] The opera house in Manaus has been completely restored and, since 2003, has played host to opera and other events.

[13] See the chapter "Dealing with the 'Successor Generation'" in Tuch, *Communicating with the World*, 152–60.

[14] See Hans N. Tuch, *Arthur Burns and the Successor Generation* (Lanham, Md.: University Press of America, 1988).

[15] For Wick's impact on USIA, see Tuch, *Communicating with the World*, 34–35.

[16] For an explanation of the reasons for this program and how it worked, see Tuch, *Arthur Burns and the Successor Generation*, 61–65.

[17] I frequently mention "Wolf Trap alumni" because, as will become clear in the last chapter of this book, the Wolf Trap Opera Company became an organization of special interest to Mimi and me.

[18] My book *Communicating with the World* served as the basis for both courses.

[19] I might note that the title of the opera caused some concern to the Opera Company. Originally entitled *Boule de Suif, or, The Good Whore* and so initially advertised, the title raised eyebrows and worse, so that the name was changed to the less provocative *The Greater Good*.

[20] When in 2007 the WTOC revived *Volpone* with a new production, Mimi and I contributed the means to create surtitles.

Index

Printed in the United States
124230LV00002B/55-111/P

9 780981 865409